contents

breakfast and brunch 3

quick snacks 63

children's meals 123

marvelous melts 184

wonderful wraps 243

comfort food 303

glossary 363

weights and measures 364

index 366

Published by: R&R Publications Marketing Pty Ltd
ACN 062 090 555
12 Edward Street, Brunswick Victoria 3056 Australia
Australia wide toll free: 1 800 063 296

Easy Recipes

Author: Brenda Kitchen
Publisher: Anthony Carroll
Food Editor: Neil Hargreaves
Graphic Designer: Aisling Gallagher
Photography: Brent Parker Jones
Food Stylist: Lee Blaylock
Recipe Development: Brenda Kitchen
Editor/Proofreader: Vanessa Battersby, Stepthen Jones

ISBN 1 74022 648 8

This edition printed January 2008

Printed in Singapore

Brenda Kitchen's

BREAKFAST & BRUNCH

On the table

in 20 minutes

contents

introduction   4

magic healing foods   6

excellent egg dishes   7

versatile vegetables   19

fabulous fish   29

choice chicken   41

marvellous meat   51

glossary   61

weights and measures   62

index   64

Introduction

Brenda Kitchen

Whenever I think of brunch I fondly remember the wonderful times I spent at Cronulla Beach, south of Sydney – annual reunions with my glamour friends from the glory days!

The kiosk at South Cronulla Beach had it all – fabulous food, friendly staff, bustling atmosphere plus a location to die for. Once an old beachside shop, it was now a thriving social hub. Locals and visitors gravitated to the busy café to enjoy time out with family and friends. The food was fast, fresh and delicious, while the coffee was simply divine. This sure-fire combination guaranteed a packed house every weekend in fine weather! For Meryl, Susie, Cherry and myself, our reunions will always hold a feast of memories – many of which owe their existence to the great times spent at this beachside kiosk. Today, most people will agree that brunch, as it's now known, is one of life's simple pleasures.

I trust you receive as much enjoyment from these easy recipes as I did when I created and wrote them. This book is one of a series of six bearing the title of "On the Table in 20 Minutes".

Cooking with feeling ~ Brenda

6

Brunch – perfect for lazy weekends!

Brunch is the one meal that virtually demands a sleep-in on Saturday or Sunday. The food you choose can be as varied as the folks who eat it.

My family and friends believe there's no better way to relax on a lazy Sunday than to catch up for brunch and tuck into creamy scrambled eggs, crispy bacon and hot buttered toast or one of the myriad flavoursome goodies on the menu. Pure decadence, I call it! Brunch is very much about socialising and enjoying good company. It's a time to forget the everyday humdrum of our busy lives. We switch off, wind down and once again become our true selves.

The recipes I've created for brunch cover a wide selection of ingredients and give you the option of either preparing them exactly as the recipe says or using them as a base to create your own work of art! For instance, I love the use of fresh herbs and believe that most recipes can be enhanced by the inclusion of finely chopped chives, parsley and thyme, either individually or in combination.

Food has always inspired my imagination

Magic
healing foods

These foods have healing powers. Eat lots of them!

Bananas	are an excellent source of potassium.
Broccoli	is an excellent source of calcium and assists calcium absorption.
Cabbage	is known to have cancer-fighting properties.
Garlic	is nature's antibiotic. It's an energy-booster for the immune system.
Potatoes	are a fantastic source of fibre.
Pumpkin	contains betacarotene, an excellent antioxidant.
Olive oil	moisturises the skin and is healthy to cook with.
Onions	purify the blood.
Spinach	is a rich source of iron and is high in vitamins and minerals.
Tomatoes	are a rich source of antioxidants.

Fat is needed in your diet. A little fat provides flavour and long-lasting satisfaction, which prevents the need to snack in between meals.

Have a creative time in the kitchen and relax by preparing early, so you can really enjoy your tasty meal

excellent egg dishes

eggs in pots

INGREDIENTS
4 large free-range eggs
100g leg ham, finely chopped
½ bunch chives, finely chopped
½ cup parsley, finely chopped
½ cup cream
salt and pepper to taste

METHOD
1 Preheat the oven to 180°C.

2 Divide the eggs, ham, chives, parsley and cream into each of the four greased ramekins.

3 Sprinkle with salt and pepper to taste. Cover each ramekin with foil and cook on a baking tray for 10 minutes or until the eggs are set.

Serves 4   Calories 243
Fat 20.9g   Preparation 6 mins
Cooking 10 mins

creamy scrambled eggs

INGREDIENTS
10 large free-range eggs
½ cup thin cream
salt and pepper to taste
1 tablespoon butter
¼ cup parsley, finely chopped, to garnish

METHOD
1 Gently whisk the eggs, cream and salt and pepper until just combined. Do not over-beat, or the mixture will toughen when cooked.

2 Melt the butter in a medium-sized pan over medium heat and add the egg mixture.

3 Using a wooden spoon, very gently stir the mixture until almost cooked. Turn off heat and cover for 2 minutes.

Serves 4   Calories 315   Fat 25.5g   Preparation 3 mins   Cooking 8 mins

creamy scrambled eggs

excellent egg dishes

Hint: Make sure the bread is sliced thickly. To enhance the flavour, add a little butter to the pan during cooking.

egg in a nest

INGREDIENTS

8 slices crusty Italian bread
2 tablespoons extra virgin olive oil
8 large free-range eggs
freshly ground black pepper
sea salt to taste

METHOD

1 Cut a hole in each of the slices of bread, about the size of a 50-cent piece. Brush one side of each slice of bread with olive oil.

2 Place the bread, oil side down, in a frying pan on medium heat.

3 Break an egg into the hole of each slice of bread. Once the egg starts to set, brush on a little oil and turn to cook the other side of the bread and complete the cooking of the egg.

4 Sprinkle with salt and pepper and serve on warm plates.

Serves 4 **Calories** 395
Fat 22.6g **Preparation** 4 mins
Cooking 8 mins

breakfast feast

INGREDIENTS

8 slices streaky bacon
4 tomatoes, halved
2 onions, thinly sliced
4 lean beef sausages
2 teaspoons white vinegar
1 tablespoon plain flour
salt and pepper to taste
8 large free-range eggs, at room
temperature
4 slices turkish bread, toasted

METHOD

1 Dry-fry the bacon and tomato pieces in a non-stick frying pan and place in a warm oven. Fry the onions in the same pan with the sausages. Cook for 8 minutes, turning a few times.

2 Meanwhile, half fill a separate large frying pan with water and bring to a simmer. Add the vinegar.

3 Sprinkle the flour over the sausages and onion, stirring well. Add ½ cup of hot water and salt and pepper to taste. Cover and simmer for 5 minutes.

4 Swirl the simmering frying pan with a large spoon, to create a gentle whirlpool motion. Crack the eggs into the centre of the water and gently swirl the water again. After the water returns to the simmer, wait 2 minutes longer and gently remove and drain the poached eggs. Serve eggs on top of Turkish bread with bacon, tomato, sauage and onion at the side.

Hint: The bacon, sausages and onion can also be served with creamy mashed potato, stir-fried cabbage and steamed carrots.

Serves 4 **Calories** 718
Fat 32.2g **Preparation** 10 mins
Cooking 20 mins

13

salmon and spinach quiche

salmon and spinach quiche

INGREDIENTS

210g canned red salmon, drained and mashed

250g light sour cream

1 small bunch spinach, green part only, lightly steamed

4 free-range eggs, lightly beaten

100g Cheddar cheese, grated

1 bunch chives, chopped

freshly ground black pepper

2 sheets pre-made puff pastry

METHOD

1 Preheat the oven to 180°C.

2 Combine the salmon, sour cream, spinach, eggs, cheese, chives and black pepper, and mix gently.

3 Line 4 individual-serving-size springform pans with pastry cut to size. Pour in the quiche mixture. Bake for 20 minutes.

eat more quiche

A really good quiche is full of flavour, satisfying and easy to make. Some years ago my friends Yvonne and Peter invited me to share a casual Sunday lunch. Like me they love food and great quality produce, and just-picked spinach from their small veggie patch was the star of this yummy quiche. Lightly steamed and finely chopped it gave great depth to this easy-to-prepare meal. To add a gourmet touch, Yvonne would sometimes add a topping of sliced vine-ripened tomatoes and a light sprinkle of freshly grated Parmesan cheese.

Sharing time with friends is one of life's great pleasures and cooking for friends creates a real sense of occasion. Food and friends – a combination that should always be on the menu!

Hint: This mixture can also be used to create one medium-sized quiche. Bake in a moderate oven for 35 minutes.

15

Serves 4 **Calories** 727 **Fat** 51.2g **Preparation** 10 mins **Cooking** 20 mins

Hint: This recipe can be cooked in an electric frying pan. Smoked trout or fresh cooked prawns also make nice additions to this recipe.

fabulous *pan frittata*

INGREDIENTS

1 tablespoon olive oil

6 large free-range eggs

⅓ cup cream

6 mushrooms, finely chopped

2 tablespoons Parmesan cheese, grated

50g Cheddar cheese, grated

1 bunch chives, chopped

½ cup parsley, chopped

100g lean ham, chopped

salt and pepper to taste

METHOD

1 Preheat oven to 180°C. Heat a small ovenproof non-stick frying pan with olive oil.

2 Combine all of the ingredients in a large bowl. Mix with a fork until just combined – do not over-beat!

3 Pour into the frying pan, reduce the heat to medium, cover and cook for 6 minutes.

4 Remove lid and place into the oven for 10 minutes. Carefully remove from pan and cut into 4 pieces and serve with a large salad.

Serves 4 **Calories** 356

Fat 29.3g **Preparation** 8 mins

Cooking 16 mins

fluffy omelette

INGREDIENTS

6 large free-range eggs
salt and pepper to taste
½ teaspoon butter
2 tomatoes, sliced
50g vintage Cheddar cheese, grated

METHOD

1 Separate the egg whites and yolks. Beat the egg whites until soft peaks form, then fold in the slightly beaten egg yolks and the salt and pepper to taste.

2 Melt the butter in a medium-sized frying pan. Spoon in the egg mixture and cook, covered, for 5 minutes over medium heat.

3 Preheat the grill to medium. Arrange slices of tomato over the top of the omelette and season with salt and pepper to taste. Sprinkle the grated cheese on top and grill the omelette until golden. Cut into 4 equal pieces and serve immediately.

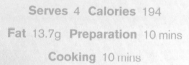

Hint: This very simple recipe was given to me by my grandmother, who cooked it as a special treat on weekends. On occasion, she would add small pieces of lean cooked bacon to the topping before the cheese.

Serves 4 **Calories** 194
Fat 13.7g **Preparation** 10 mins
Cooking 10 mins

tasty green omelette

tasty green omelette

INGREDIENTS

12 large free-range eggs

2 tablespoons cream

small bunch chives, finely chopped

¼ cup parsley, finely chopped, plus extra to garnish

freshly ground black pepper and sea salt

2 tablespoons butter

6 button mushrooms, diced

100g vintage Cheddar cheese, grated

METHOD

1 Combine the eggs, cream, chives, parsley and salt and pepper. Whisk lightly but do not over-beat.

2 Heat half of the butter in an omelette pan over medium heat. Pour half the egg mixture into the pan. Tilt the pan so the omelette covers the base, then gently draw the mixture into the centre of the pan. Tilt the pan again, so the uncooked mixture runs to the edge.

3 Place half the mushrooms and cheese onto one side of the omelette. Fold the other side of the omelette over to enclose the filling.

4 Cover and cook on low heat for 3 minutes. Set aside and keep warm. Repeat all steps to make a second omelette.

Hint: Make your own special combination – why not try tomato, ham, asparagus or cooked bacon in this recipe.

Serves 4 Calories 472 Fat 38.6g Preparation 10 mins Cooking 6 mins

19

excellent egg dishes

Hint: 100g of chopped smoked ham, smoked trout or tiny cooked prawns can be used to vary this recipe. Fresh chopped asparagus can also be included.

Makes 12 **Calories** 244
Fat 20.6g **Preparation** 15 mins
Cooking 20 mins

tasty quiche parcels

INGREDIENTS

60g baby spinach leaves
6 large free-range eggs
½ cup cream
½ cup parsley, finely chopped
100g vintage Cheddar cheese, grated
1 small red onion, finely chopped
salt and pepper to taste
12 slices truss tomato

METHOD

1 Preheat the oven to 190°C.

2 Line a muffin tray with baking paper and place some spinach leaves into each cavity, keeping some of the spinach for later. Combine the eggs, cream, parsley, grated cheese, onion and salt and pepper to taste and whisk gently. Pour equal amounts of the egg mixture into the 12 spinach-lined cavities, and top each one with the remaining spinach and a slice of tomato. Bake for 15–18 minutes or until set.

3 Serve in the baking paper as part of a brunch buffet.

versatile vegetables

versatile vegetables

Hint: For a brunch buffet, serve the garlic bruschetta with an antipasto platter of cold meats, cheeses and a variety of marinated vegetables.

Hint: Add sliced onion and 100g of chopped smoked bacon when frying the mushrooms to make an even tastier, more substantial meal.

bruschetta varieties

INGREDIENTS

8 slices crusty Italian-style bread
1 tablespoon olive oil
1 teaspoon butter, melted
2 cloves garlic, crushed
¼ cup parsley, finely chopped
salt and pepper to taste

toppings

semi-sun-dried tomatoes, char-grilled eggplant, roasted red capsicum, pitted black olives, torn basil leaves

Serves 4 **Calories** 169
Fat 6.9g **Preparation** 8 mins
Cooking 6 mins

METHOD

1 Preheat the grill to medium-high.

2 Combine olive oil, melted butter, garlic, parsley and salt and pepper to taste.

3 Brush on side of each slice of bread with the oil and butter mixture and grill that side until golden and fragrant.

4 Serve topped with a little of each of the suggested toppings. Add salt and pepper to taste.

breakfast mushrooms

INGREDIENTS

3 tablespoons butter
500g field mushrooms, sliced
2 teaspoons plain flour
½ cup milk
small bunch chives, chopped
salt and pepper to taste
4 thick slices sourdough bread, toasted

METHOD

1 Heat a non-stick frying pan on a medium heat.

2 Melt the butter in the frying pan and add the mushrooms. Cook for a few minutes until the mushrooms soften.

3 Add plain flour and stir through the mushrooms. Add the milk and the chopped chives, season to taste and serve on hot buttered toast for a yummy breakfast!

Serves 4 **Calories** 264 **Fat** 14.2g **Preparation** 4 mins **Cooking** 8 mins

versatile vegetables

Hint: Serve this traditional Italian salad with crusty bread and smoked meats, chicken or crispy grilled bacon.

Serves 4 **Calories** 339
Fat 29.4g **Preparation** 4 mins

caprese salad

INGREDIENTS

4 ripe truss tomatoes, sliced thickly

200g buffalo-milk Mozzarella cheese, sliced

fresh basil leaves

4 tablespoons good-quality extra virgin cold-pressed olive oil

freshly ground black pepper and salt

METHOD

1 Place slices of tomato onto a serving tray and top with the buffalo-milk Mozzarella cheese and fresh basil leaves. Drizzle the olive oil over the salad and season well with salt and pepper.

fetta, olive and oregano muffins

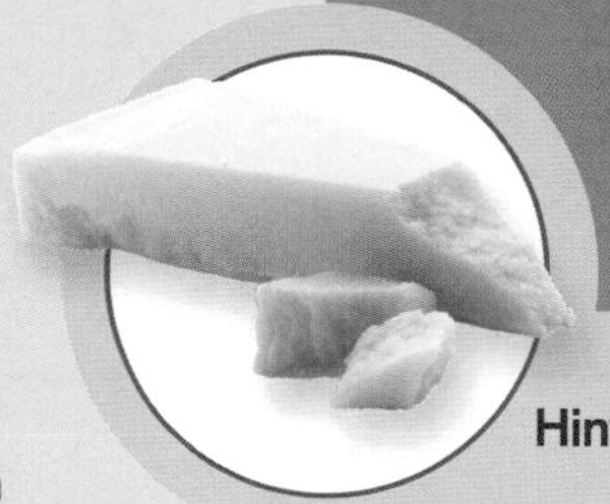

INGREDIENTS

2½ cups self-raising flour

100g fetta cheese, crumbled

50g Parmesan cheese, grated

2 eggs

1 cup milk

½ cup fresh oregano leaves, chopped

2 tablespoons butter, softened

ground black pepper and sea salt to taste

1 cup black olives, chopped

METHOD

1 Preheat the oven to 180°C. Combine all of the ingredients in a large bowl and mix with a wooden spoon – do not over-beat the mixture. Spoon the mixture into a 12-muffin tray and bake for 15–18 minutes.

Hint: Serve these muffins with butter and tomato relish. Finely chopped semi-sun-dried tomato and chopped jalapeños can be added to this recipe – or poke a cube of tasty vintage Cheddar cheese into the centre of each muffin prior to baking.

Makes 12 **Calories** 408

Fat 16.4g **Preparation** 4 mins

Cooking 18 mins

versatile vegetables

Hint: Fresh torn basil, oregano or thyme can be included in this simple recipe.

Serves 4 Calories 872
Fat 32g Preparation 10 mins
Cooking 15 mins

linguini with breadcrumbs

INGREDIENTS

2 cups stale breadcrumbs
½ cup extra virgin olive oil
2 onions, finely chopped
3 cloves garlic, crushed
2 x 400g canned chopped tomatoes
½ cup flat-leaf parsley, chopped
½ cup black olives, chopped
2 tablespoons capers
1 teaspoon chilli flakes
salt and pepper to taste
500g linguini, cooked

METHOD

1 Fry the breadcrumbs in half of the oil until golden and set aside. Fry the onion and garlic in the remaining oil until soft, and add the tomatoes. Simmer for 15 minutes.

2 Add the parsley, olives, chilli flakes and seasonings, capers, and toss to combine. Combine the cooked linguini and the sauce. Divide the mixture between 4 bowls and sprinkle with breadcrumbs.

savoury tart

INGREDIENTS

2 large brown onions, thinly sliced
1 tablespoon butter
1 teaspoon brown sugar
1 teaspoon red wine vinegar
1 sheet pre-made puff pastry
100g Cheddar cheese, grated
½ cup sage leaves

METHOD

1 Preheat the oven to 200°C.

2 Gently fry the onions in butter for 15 minutes until soft and golden, then add the sugar and vinegar and cook for 5 minutes. Line a lamington tin with the pastry and spread the onion mixture over the top.

3 Sprinkle with the cheese and sage leaves, then bake for 15–18 minutes. Serve sliced with a simple green salad.

Hint: Create a double quantity of the cooked onion mixture ahead of time – it can also be used as a part of pizza toppings or bruschetta toppings.

Serves 4 **Calories** 324
Fat 21.9g **Preparation** 10 mins
Cooking 20 mins

Hint: Grilled field mushrooms and tomatoes sautéed in a little olive oil can be served as an accompaniment to the scrambled tofu.

Serves 4 **Calories** 234
Fat 11.9g **Preparation** 5 mins
Cooking 6 mins

scrambled tofu

INGREDIENTS

6 button mushrooms, quartered
½ red capsicum, finely diced
1 teaspoon olive oil
½ bunch chives, finely chopped
½ cup parsley, finely chopped
350g firm tofu, crumbled
1 tablespoon tamari
freshly ground black pepper
and sea salt to taste
4 slices buttered toast to serve

METHOD

1 Lightly fry the mushrooms and capsicum in the olive oil for 3 minutes, then add the chives and parsley, crumbled tofu, tamari and salt and pepper to taste. Stir-fry gently for about 3 minutes. Serve on buttered toast.

tofu burgers

INGREDIENTS

350g firm tofu
1 tablespoon olive oil
1 clove garlic, crushed
2 teaspoons ground cumin
salt and pepper to taste
4 tablespoons hummus
50g mixed salad leaves
1 red capsicum, finely chopped
4 slices crusty bread or bread rolls

METHOD

1 Cut tofu into 4 even slices.

2 Combine oil, garlic, cumin and seasoning in a bowl. Dip tofu slices in the mix and coat well. Pan-fry the tofu until heated through 2 minutes each side.

3 Serve on crusty bread or a bread roll spread with hummus, top with mixed salad leaves and the chopped capsicum.

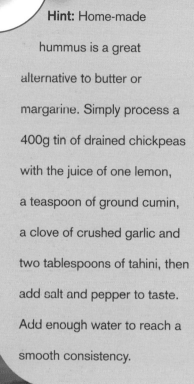

Hint: Home-made hummus is a great alternative to butter or margarine. Simply process a 400g tin of drained chickpeas with the juice of one lemon, a teaspoon of ground cumin, a clove of crushed garlic and two tablespoons of tahini, then add salt and pepper to taste. Add enough water to reach a smooth consistency.

Serves 4 **Calories** 288
Fat 15.3g **Preparation** 12 mins
Cooking 6 mins

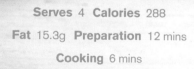

29

versatile vegetables

Hint: Rich red truss tomatoes, parsley and coriander can be used to replace the Roma tomatoes and basil here. The bread should always be thick-cut, crusty Italian-style bread.

Serves 4 **Calories** 238
Fat 7.2g **Preparation** 8 mins
Cooking 4 mins

traditional bruschetta

INGREDIENTS
6 Roma tomatoes, finely chopped
1 large red onion, finely chopped
10 leaves basil, torn
2 teaspoons red wine vinegar
salt and pepper to taste
3 tablespoons extra virgin olive oil
4 cloves garlic, crushed
2 teaspoons butter, softened
¼ cup parsley, finely chopped
10 slices sourdough bread

METHOD
1 Gently combine in a glass bowl, the Roma tomatoes, onion, basil, vinegar, salt and pepper and 2 tablespoons of the oil.

2 Combine the garlic, butter, parsley and the remaining oil. Brush the slices of sourdough with this mixture and grill until golden.

3 Serve the tomato mixture and garlic bread separately, allowing guests to create their own tasty bruschetta.

fabulous
fish

Hint: Freeze the uncooked patties for up to 2 months and you'll have healthy food on hand for fussy kids!

cheesy salmon patties

INGREDIENTS

440g canned pink salmon, mashed with the liquid

50g cheese, grated

1 cup rice, cooked

1 cup cold mashed potato

1 egg

small bunch chives, chopped

½ cup fresh parsley, finely chopped

1 cup dried breadcrumbs

1 tablespoon olive oil

1 teaspoon butter

Serves 4 Calories 498

Fat 20.7g Preparation 10 mins

Cooking 8 mins

METHOD

1 Combine the first seven ingredients and form into small balls or patties.

2 Coat with breadcrumbs and fry in combined oil and butter for about 4 minutes each side on a medium heat, until golden.

Hint: Toss the rocket with a little red wine vinegar and good quality olive oil plus freshly ground black pepper and sea salt.

light baked fish

INGREDIENTS

4 boneless fish fillets

1 cup multigrain breadcrumbs

50g Parmesan cheese, grated

¾ cup parsley, finely chopped

1 teaspoon lemon zest

2 teaspoons olive oil

salt and pepper to taste

METHOD

1 Preheat the oven to 200°C.

2 Line a baking tray with baking paper and place the fish on the baking paper.

3 Combine the breadcrumbs, Parmesan cheese, parsley, lemon zest, olive oil and salt and pepper to taste. Mix well, coat each fish fillet with crumb mixture and bake for 12–15 minutes. Serve with a simple rocket salad.

Serves 4 Calories 353 Fat 11g Preparation 10 mins Cooking 15 mins

fabulous fish

Hint: This recipe is suitable for buffet-style entertaining or casual dining and can be cooked ahead of time and reheated in a microwave or regular oven – just cover to reheat! Steamed smoked cod can be substituted for the salmon or fish.

Serves 4 **Calories** 411
Fat 14g **Preparation** 10 mins
Cooking 5 mins

kind of kedgeree

INGREDIENTS

1 large onion, chopped
2 cloves garlic, crushed
1 tablespoon olive oil
2 teaspoons curry powder
3 cups jasmine rice, cooked
1 cup cooked boneless fish
or 300g pink salmon
juice of 1 lemon
½ cup parsley, freshly chopped
salt and freshly ground black
pepper to taste
3 hard-boiled eggs
½ cup coriander, freshly chopped

METHOD

1 Cook the onion and garlic in olive oil until softened. Add the curry powder and stir to combine.

2 Add rice, fish, lemon juice and parsley. Season to taste.

3 Place into a shallow casserole dish, top with sliced hard-boiled eggs and chopped coriander.

4 Serve with a big, healthy salad and crusty bread.

smoked trout salad

INGREDIENTS

200g smoked trout, diced

6 new potatoes, steamed and quartered

80g rocket

80g iceberg lettuce, roughly torn

1 punnet grape tomatoes, halved

½ cup shallots, chopped

½ red capsicum, thinly sliced

1 tablespoon extra virgin olive oil

2 teaspoons lemon juice

1 teaspoon honey

salt and pepper to taste

METHOD

1 Dry-fry the trout quickly until crisp and set aside. Toss the cooked potatoes in the same pan.

2 In a large salad bowl, toss the rocket, lettuce, tomatoes, shallots and capsicum.

3 Combine the olive oil, lemon juice and honey and add to the salad. Add the potato and trout at the last minute.

4 Season and serve with toasted rye bread.

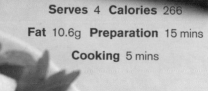

Hint: Warm salads are a wonderful way to combine healthy, crisp greens with small cooked pieces of lamb, chicken, beef, pork or seafood.

Serves 4 **Calories** 266

Fat 10.6g **Preparation** 15 mins

Cooking 5 mins

tasty tuna and mini penne

tasty tuna *and mini penne*

INGREDIENTS

1 red onion, finely chopped
2 cloves garlic, crushed
1 teaspoon butter
2 teaspoons olive oil
1 cup mushrooms, chopped
2 tomatoes, chopped
½ cup parsley, chopped
salt and pepper to taste
squeeze of lemon juice
200g canned tuna in olive oil
1 teaspoon oregano leaves
6 cups mini penne, cooked
100g Parmesan cheese, grated
100g Cheddar cheese, grated

METHOD

1 Preheat the oven to 180°C and grease a medium-sized casserole dish.

2 Fry the onion and garlic in the butter and olive oil until soft.

3 Add the mushrooms, tomato, parsley, salt and pepper, lemon juice, tuna with oil and oregano leaves. Cook for 3 minutes then add the pasta.

4 Place the pasta mixture into the casserole dish, top with cheese and bake for 20 minutes in a moderate oven.

Serves 4 **Calories** 689 **Fat** 32.3g **Preparation** 8 mins **Cooking** 25 mins

fasta pasta

Pasta is a universal favourite and most of us can name at least one pasta dish we can't resist. Some years ago, my favourite Italian restaurant closed forever and I was devastated! Looking forward to a tasty lunch, my friend and I made our way to the humble restaurant. You can imagine our disappointment at finding it closed, boarded up, and looking very neglected. This Italian landmark started its life as a simple café in the 70s. What a shame to see its demise – very sad!

One dish that I loved was a very simple blend of pasta with tuna, olive oil, garlic and pepper. It was most likely tinned tuna packed in extra virgin olive oil and the pasta was mini penne – a perfect combination. I was therefore thrilled to find a good quality mini penne in the supermarket, along with Italian-style tuna in extra virgin olive oil – so easy yet so good!

Hint: Cooked chicken breast, a leg ham or tin of salmon can also be used in this recipe.

fabulous fish

smoked trout pasta

Hint: Smoked salmon or cooked prawns can be used in this recipe.

Serves 4 **Calories** 598
Fat 43.8g **Preparation** 8 mins
Cooking 8 mins

INGREDIENTS

1 small red onion, chopped
1 clove garlic, crushed
1 teaspoon butter
1 tablespoon olive oil
6 button mushrooms, sliced
100g fillet smoked trout, diced
½ cup parsley, chopped
¼ cup dill, chopped
300mL cream
black pepper to taste
3 cups mini penne, cooked
50g Parmesan cheese, grated

METHOD

1 Sauté onion and garlic in butter and oil until soft but not brown. Add mushrooms and cook for a few minutes only.

2 Add the trout, parsley, dill, cream and pepper. Simmer for a few minutes.

3 Stir the sauce through the hot cooked pasta and serve with the grated Parmesan cheese.

tasty fish mornay

INGREDIENTS

4 boneless fish fillets, with a light
sprinkle of Thai seasoning

2 teaspoons butter

2 teaspoons plain flour

½ cup milk

50g Parmesan cheese, grated

freshly ground black pepper to taste

¼ cup fresh parsley, finely chopped

50g Cheddar cheese, grated

METHOD

1 Gently fry fish in butter for 2 minutes each side. Remove from pan and set aside.

2 Sprinkle flour into pan and stir well with a wooden spoon until smooth. Add milk, stirring until thickened. (Add a little more milk if the sauce is too thick.)

3 Add Parmesan cheese, pepper and parsley. Place fish in sauce and spoon over a little of the sauce to cover each fillet. Sprinkle with grated Cheddar cheese.

4 To brown the cheese you may either place the frying pan directly under the grill or place the mixture in a serving dish that can be placed under the grill.

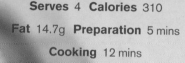

Hint: For a gourmet touch, add a few small cooked prawns to each fish fillet and then spoon over the mornay sauce.

Serves 4 **Calories** 310
Fat 14.7g **Preparation** 5 mins
Cooking 12 mins

smoked salmon bagel

smoked salmon bagel

INGREDIENTS

4 tablespoons light cream cheese

freshly ground black pepper

2 teaspoons horseradish cream

100g smoked salmon

1 lime

4 bagels

1 red onion, sliced

2 teaspoons capers

60g mixed lettuce leaves

½ cup cherry tomatoes, halved

METHOD

1 Combine the cream cheese, black pepper and horseradish cream and mix well.

2 Separate the smoked salmon slices and squeeze over the juice of half the lime.

3 Toast the halved bagels and spread the cream cheese mixture onto each one. Top with slices of smoked salmon, red onion slices and a few capers.

4 Toss the lettuce and tomatoes with a squeeze of lime and serve as an accompaniment to the salmon bagels.

Hint: Wasabi or mustard are two wonderful flavours and can be used to replace the horseradish cream, giving you alternatives that still match the flavour of the salmon.

Serves 4 **Calories** 337 **Fat** 6.1g **Preparation** 4 mins **Cooking** 4 mins

41

tuna and watercress salad

Hint: For a quick alternative dressing for this salad use:

¼ cup extra virgin olive oil

1 tablespoon lemon juice

1 tablespoon honey. Shake to combine in a small screw-top glass jar.

INGREDIENTS

200g fresh tuna
1 teaspoon extra virgin olive oil
1 tablespoon apple cider vinegar
¼ cup walnut oil
1 teaspoon tamari
freshly ground black pepper
1 cup watercress, tender tips only
10 cherry tomatoes, halved
1 cup bean shoots
½ cup walnut halves
½ cup shallots, finely chopped

METHOD

1 Fry the tuna in the olive oil for 2 minutes each side. Allow to rest whilst you make the salad.

2 To make the dressing, combine apple cider vinegar, walnut oil, tamari and freshly ground black pepper.

3 Combine the watercress, tomatoes, bean shoots, walnuts and shallots in a salad bowl. Top with the diced tuna and the dressing.

Serves 4 **Calories** 322
Fat 27.5g **Preparation** 10 mins
Cooking 4 mins

choice
chicken

choice chicken

Hint: As an alternative, omit the soy sauce and bean sprouts. Add ½ cup of crumbled fetta cheese and ¼ cup of chopped black olives.

Hint: This recipe is especially easy to make, with the bonus of being not only tasty but also very healthy.

chicken and ham fritters

INGREDIENTS

4 free-range eggs
1 cup chicken, cooked
1 cup ham, finely chopped
½ cup parsley, finely chopped
½ cup shallots, finely chopped
½ cup plain flour
2 teaspoons soy sauce
1 cup bean sprouts
oil for frying

Serves 4 Calories 428
Fat 29.6g Preparation 8 mins
Cooking 4 mins

METHOD

1 Combine all of the ingredients in a large bowl.

2 Cook heaped tablespoons of the mixture in hot oil until golden, about 2 minutes. Turn and repeat.

3 Serve with a mild chilli sauce and honey.

famous chicken sesame burgers

INGREDIENTS

1 medium carrot, grated
1 medium onion, finely diced
1 cup parsley, finely chopped
½ cup basil, finely chopped
1 tablespoon dried mixed herbs
1 tablespoon tamari
250g chicken mince
1 tablespoon extra virgin olive oil

METHOD

1 Preheat oven to 200°C. Combine all of the ingredients except the oil. Mix well to combine.

2 Fry large patties of mixture in a little hot olive oil – flatten burgers in frying pan. Turn and cook the other side. Place in oven for 8 minutes.

3 Serve on toasted grain roll with fresh salad ingredients and sauce of your choice.

Serves 4 Calories 150 Fat 9.7g Preparation 10 mins Cooking 12 mins

famous chicken sesame burgers

crustless chicken, pumpkin and spinach pi

Hint: This can be a great side dish for your next barbecue or main course. To create a savoury crumble topping for this recipe, simply combine 1 cup of Cheddar cheese, ½ cup of fresh breadcrumbs, 2 teaspoons of oregano leaves and a few chilli flakes.

Serves 4 **Calories** 479
Fat 33.3g **Preparation** 10 mins
Cooking 18 mins

INGREDIENTS

1 large onion, finely chopped
3 cloves garlic, crushed
1 bunch spinach, lightly steamed
oil for frying
pinch of nutmeg
ground pepper and sea salt to taste
1 cup pumpkin, grated
400g chicken thighs, finely diced
4 large eggs
½ cup light cream
100g Cheddar cheese, grated
½ teaspoon ground paprika

METHOD

1 Preheat the oven to 200°C and grease 4 small ramekins.

2 Lightly fry the onion, garlic and the cooked, drained and chopped spinach in a little olive oil. Add seasonings, pumpkin and chicken. Divide the mixture among the ramekins.

3 Combine the eggs, cream and cheese and pour over the spinach mixture. Sprinkle with paprika and cover with foil.

4 Bake for 18 minutes or until golden brown.

chicken croquette salad

INGREDIENTS

- 500g chicken mince
- 1 egg
- salt and pepper to taste
- 1 teaspoon mixed herbs
- 1 red onion, finely diced
- 1 teaspoon chilli flakes
- 2 cups dry, fine breadcrumbs
- ½ cup peanut oil
- 1 cos lettuce, washed and torn into bite-sized pieces
- 1 punnet grape tomatoes, halved
- ½ cup shallots, chopped
- 1 Lebanese cucumber, thinly sliced
- juice of 1 lemon
- 2 teaspoons olive oil

METHOD

1 Combine the chicken mince, egg, salt and pepper, mixed herbs, red onion and chilli flakes. Chill the mixture for 15 minutes.

2 Roll tablespoons of the mixture in breadcrumbs and form into a small sausage shape. Fry in peanut oil over medium heat until golden, turning a few times. The cooking time will depend upon the size of the croquettes.

3 Serve on a bed of lettuce, tomato, shallots and cucumber that has been tossed with the lemon juice and olive oil.

Hint: Whole-egg mayonnaise or sweet chilli sauce make a good accompaniment to this dish.

Serves 4 Calories 751
Fat 44.9g Preparation 25 mins
Cooking 15 mins

47

Hint: Why not try substituting the chicken with lean leg ham or cooked school prawns?

Serves 4 Calories 959
Fat 59g Preparation 20 mins
Cooking 15 mins

baked chicken and mushroom crepes

INGREDIENTS

Crepes

2 eggs, lightly beaten

1⅔ cups milk

2 cups plain flour

pinch salt

1 tablespoon butter, melted

Filling

6 button mushrooms, sliced

1 tablespoon butter

2 cups chicken breast fillet, cooked and diced

1 cup cream

150g Swiss cheese, grated

small bunch chives, finely chopped

salt and pepper to taste

METHOD

1 To make the crepes, mix the eggs and milk together and add ½ cup of water. Sift the flour and the salt, and whisk in the liquid to form a smooth batter. Add the melted butter and stir to combine. Cover and place in the refrigerator for 10 minutes.

2 Cook the crepes one at a time for about 1 minute each side in a non-stick pan on moderate heat. Place a piece of greaseproof paper between each crepe.

3 To fill the crepes, preheat to 180°C. Fry the mushrooms in butter until soft then add the chicken breast pieces, cream, cheese, chives and salt and pepper to taste. Stir to combine. Place 2 tablerspoons of mixture onto each crepe and roll up to enclose the filling. Place on a baking tray lined with baking paper and bake for 5 minutes.

hunza chicken bake

INGREDIENTS

1 cup jasmine rice, cooked
1 medium onion, chopped
1 bunch silverbeet, chopped
200g low-fat cheese, grated
300g chicken thighs
sprinkle of nutmeg
salt and pepper to taste
½ cup dried breadcrumbs
¼ cup fresh parsley, chopped
1 tomato, sliced

METHOD

1 Preheat the oven to 210°C and grease a casserole dish.

2 Add half the chopped onion and silverbeet in a casserole dish and cover and cook in a microwave for 3 minutes. Remove the mixture and set aside. Cook the remaining onion and silverbeet in the same way.

3 Stir in half the cheese, the jasmines rice, the chicken pieces and a sprinkle of nutmeg and salt and pepper to taste.

4 Press the remaining mixture down into the casserole dish, season again and top with breadcrumbs, remaining grated cheese, chopped parsley and tomato slices. Bake for approximately 20 minutes.

Hint: You can also create a tasty pie by lining a pie dish with wholemeal pre-made pastry and spooning the filling onto the pastry.

Serves 4 **Calories** 354
Fat 10g **Preparation** 8 mins
Cooking 20 mins

Hint: The slow cooking of the breast fillets will ensure they remain moist and tasty.

lemon and garlic chicken

INGREDIENTS

1 tablespoon olive oil

2 teaspoons butter

2 cloves garlic, crushed

2 chicken breast fillets, divided into 4 half-breast fillets

1 tablespoon lemon juice

125g mixed baby lettuce leaves

1 small onion, finely sliced

8 grape tomatoes, halved

salt and pepper to taste

METHOD

1 In a medium-sized frying pan on medium heat, add the olive oil and butter. Add the garlic and chicken.

2 Cook the chicken, cover, and reduce the heat. Turn the chicken once during the cooking time. Cook for 4 minutes per side. Add the lemon juice to the pan.

3 Combine the mixed baby lettuce leaves, onion and grape tomatoes in a bowl. Add the pan juices to the salad. Season and divide the salad between 4 serving plates, top with a sliced breast fillet and serve.

Serves 4 **Calories** 388

Fat 25.6g **Preparation** 5 mins

Cooking 12 mins

quesadillas

INGREDIENTS

250g chicken breast fillet strips

1 tablespoon olive oil

25g burrito seasoning mix

½ cup light sour cream

½ cup tomato salsa

8 medium tortillas

50g lettuce, shredded

2 tomatoes, finely chopped

100g Cheddar cheese, grated

salt and pepper to taste

METHOD

1 Preheat a café-style sandwich press.

2 Gently fry the chicken breast strips in the olive oil for 4 minutes. Add the burrito seasoning, stir and cook for 3 minutes. Add the sour cream and the salsa. Simmer for 5 minutes.

3 Divide the mixture between 4 tortillas, top with lettuce, chopped tomato, grated cheese and salt and pepper to taste. Top with another tortilla and cook one at a time in the sandwich press until crisp, about 4 minutes. Cut into wedges to serve.

Hint: Lean pork, veal and beef strips can also be used in this recipe.

Serves 4 **Calories** 456
Fat 25.8g **Preparation** 8 mins
Cooking 20 mins

chicken and vegetable slice

Hint: This recipe is a great way to use up small amounts of vegetables that might otherwise be discarded!

Serves 4 Calories 570
Fat 18.5g Preparation 8 mins
Cooking 20 mins

INGREDIENTS

400g chicken breast, diced
2 large zucchini, grated
2 large carrots, peeled and grated
2 large onions, finely chopped
1 cup parsley, finely chopped
50g Cheddar cheese, grated
2 large free-range eggs
½ cup plain flour
salt and pepper to taste
4 tomatoes, sliced
50g Parmesan cheese, grated
4 large sebago potatoes, peeled and grated

METHOD

1 Preheat the oven to 200°C.

2 Combine the chicken, grated vegetables, onion, parsley, cheese, eggs, flour and salt and pepper to taste. Pour the mixture into 4 individual mini-loaf pans, then top with slices of tomato and sprinkle with grated Parmesan cheese. Bake for 20 minutes. Serve with a crisp green salad.

marvellous
meat

marvellous meat

Hint: After topping the toasted sandwich with cheese, place under a preheated grill and cook until golden. This works well for cooking 4–6 sandwiches. You can even make these a little ahead of time and finish the cooking under the grill as required.

Hint: Leftover Bolognese sauce can be used instead of the pasta sauce for a very tasty alternative.

french sandwich

INGREDIENTS
100g butter, softened
8 thick slices white bread
200g leg ham, sliced
2 teaspoons mild American mustard
100g Cheddar cheese, grated
bunch fresh chives, finely chopped
salt and pepper to taste

Serves 4 Calories 497
Fat 32.5g Preparation 5 mins
Cooking 8 mins

METHOD
1 Heat an electric frying pan on high. Butter slices of bread, and add them buttered side down.

2 Add ham, mustard, a sprinkle of grated cheese, fresh chives and salt and pepper to taste. Cook on both sides until golden brown.

3 Top with a little grated cheese, cover and allow the cheese to melt.

cheese-topped ravioli

INGREDIENTS
500g beef ravioli
1½ cups pasta sauce
4 tomatoes, sliced
50g Parmesan cheese, grated
50g Cheddar cheese, grated
1 teaspoon dried oregano leaves
½ cup dried breadcrumbs
salt and pepper to taste

METHOD
1 Preheat the oven to 200°C. Cook the ravioli according to the directions on the packet.

2 Drain pasta well and place into a lasagne dish. Top with pasta sauce and sliced tomato.

3 Combine the two varieties of cheese, the oregano leaves and breadcrumbs, then add salt and pepper to taste.

4 Sprinkle the cheese mixture over the tomatoes and bake for 15–20 minutes. Serve with a simple rocket and lemon juice salad.

Serves 4 Calories 397 Fat 27.3g Preparation 5 mins Cooking 20 mins

cheese topped ravioli

Hint: This old-fashioned favourite is best made with chunky home-cooked corned beef.

Serves 4 **Calories** 270
Fat 11.2g **Preparation** 8 mins
Cooking 18 mins

corned beef hash

INGREDIENTS

2 teaspoons butter

1 large onion, chopped

4 medium old potatoes, peeled and finely diced

250g corned beef, cooked and chopped

¼ cup fresh parsley

salt and pepper to taste

3 large fresh eggs, beaten

METHOD

1 Heat the butter in medium sized non-stick frying pan on a medium heat. Add the onion and cook until softened.

2 Add the diced potato and cook until tender. Add the corned beef, parsley and salt and pepper to taste. Stir thoroughly, add the beaten eggs, cover and cook until firm.

3 Cut into 4 wedges, turn with an egg lifter and cook uncovered until both sides are golden brown.

baked meatballs

INGREDIENTS

500g lean beef mince

1 onion, finely chopped

1 egg

25g Parmesan cheese, grated

2 teaspoons dried oregano leaves

½ cup dried multigrain breadcrumbs

salt and pepper to taste

500g pasta sauce

100g Mozzarella cheese, sliced

1 cup basil leaves, torn

METHOD

1 Preheat the oven to 200°C.

2 Combine the mince, onion, egg, Parmesan cheese, oregano, breadcrumbs, salt and pepper to taste. Mix well and form into meatballs, a little smaller than a golf ball.

3 Dry-fry meatballs in a non-stick frying pan until brown, about 5 minutes. Transfer to a shallow lasagne dish and pour over the pasta sauce. Place the Mozzarella cheese and basil on top and bake for 15 minutes.

Hint: Make your own tomato sauce or find your favourite flavour by experimenting with several of the quality varieties from the deli or supermarket.

Serves 4 **Calories** 615

Fat 39.9g **Preparation** 15 mins

Cooking 20 mins

lamb's fry and bacon

lamb's *fry and bacon*

INGREDIENTS

1 lamb's fry, soaked in water with
a little salt for 20 minutes
½ cup plain flour, plus
1 tablespoon of plain flour
1 tablespoon olive oil
2 teaspoons butter
200g lean bacon, thinly sliced
1 large onion, peeled and sliced
salt and pepper to taste

METHOD

1 Slice lamb's fry into pieces about the thickness of a finger. Coat in ½ cup flour and fry briefly in the combined olive oil and butter – about 2 minutes each side. Place in a warm oven.

3 Fry the bacon and onion in the same pan on medium heat for 10 minutes. Sprinkle the tablespoon of plain flour over the bacon and onion mixture. Add ¾ cup of hot water and salt and pepper to taste. Stir until thickened.

4 Return the lamb's fry to the pan, cover and simmer for 5 minutes. Serve on hot buttered toast.

old food is new again

Some of the most stylish cafés and restaurants serve offal cooked in a variety of ways. My grandmother had her specialities – golden crumbed brains, home-made brawn and lamb's fry and bacon. As kids, my brother and I loved the flavours of the cleverly prepared offal. We most likely didn't know what we were eating – just that it tasted fantastic!

These days many people don't like to prepare offal at home, but they'll order it in a restaurant. Historically, offal has been cheap and available in most butcher shops. Your local butcher will sell a selection of offal too, so if you haven't cooked it before, why not give it a go? You will be preparing a meal usually only seen in restaurants these days.

Hint: Don't overcook the lamb's fry, as this will toughen it.

Serves 4 **Calories** 357 **Fat** 16.1g **Preparation** 6 mins **Cooking** 20 mins

59

marvellous meat

german sausage and roesti

Hint: Place the grated potato into a clean tea towel and squeeze out all of the moisture before mixing with the other ingredients.

Serves 4 **Calories** 728
Fat 57.1g **Preparation** 15 mins
Cooking 20 mins

INGREDIENTS

4 medium sebago potatoes, peeled and grated

1 large onion, finely chopped

½ cup parsley, finely chopped

1 egg

1 tablespoon plain flour

salt and pepper to taste

½ cup olive oil

8 weiswurst sausages

4 truss tomatoes, halved

METHOD

1 Combine the potatoes, onion, parsley, egg, flour and salt and pepper in a large bowl, and mix well with a wooden spoon.

2 Heat half of the oil over a medium heat and fry heaped tablespoons of mixture for 3–4 minutes each side. Only cook 4 at once. Keep warm in a low-heat oven. Repeat with second half pf potato mixture and oil.

3 Cut 6 diagonal cuts in the top of each sausage and fry over medium heat in a little oil until golden. Lightly fry the tomato halves.

4 Serve 2 each of the sausages, potato cakes and tomato halves per person.

potato and bacon turkish

INGREDIENTS

4 medium sebago potatoes, peeled

4 slices Turkish bread

1 tablespoon extra virgin olive oil

salt and pepper to taste

4 rashers rindless smoked bacon, chopped

½ red onion, chopped

METHOD

1 Steam the potatoes until cooked but still a little firm, and slice thinly.

2 Toast Turkish bread and brush with a little olive oil. Cut into slices and top with potato slices, salt and pepper to taste, chopped bacon and red onion. Drizzle with a little olive oil and grill until the bacon becomes crisp.

Hint: Sprinkle with grated Parmesan or Cheddar cheese prior to grilling. This recipe also works well with a pre-made pizza base.

Serves 4 **Calories** 419
Fat 15.6g **Preparation** 5 mins
Cooking 12 mins

61

potato and beef rissoles

Hint: Try baking this mixture in a greased loaf tin for 35 minutes at 180°C. Serve slices of the meatloaf either hot with vegetables or cold on a crusty roll with salad – ideal for lunch boxes!

INGREDIENTS

1 large potato, peeled and grated
1 large onion, peeled and grated
500g lean beef mince
1 tablespoon balsamic vinegar
1 tablespoon tomato salsa
1 egg
⅔ cup dried breadcrumbs
1 tablespoon oregano
½ cup fresh parsley, chopped
salt and pepper to taste
plain flour
1 tablespoon olive oil

METHOD

1 Combine all of the ingredients (except the plain flour and olive oil), shape into rissoles and coat with plain flour.

2 Place into an medium-sized frying pan and cook in olive oil until golden, about 4 minutes on each side.

Serves 4 **Calories** 366
Fat 15.6g **Preparation** 15 mins
Cooking 8 mins

Brenda Kitchen's

QUICK SNACKS

On the table

in 20 minutes

R&R PUBLICATIONS MARKETING PTY LTD

contents

introduction 66

various vegetarian 69

seafood selection 81

chicken delight 91

pork and bacon 103

lamb and beef 113

Introduction
Quick Snacks

Tasty home-made finger food can elevate your casual get-together or special celebration to a whole new level.

My friends love my home-made snacks, and are always requesting the recipes, so this Quick Snacks book is very timely. Many people are time-poor these days and believe that ready-made products are their only option, but with a little planning and my easy recipes you can produce a range of very tasty and interesting snack foods.

A selection of muffin trays in different sizes can help in the creation of bite-sized snacks. I use the mini trays to make shortcrust pastry cases for savoury fillings, while the medium-sized muffin trays can be used to make mini pizzas with the help of pre-made puff pastry.

I trust you receive as much enjoyment from using this book as I did when I created and wrote these easy recipes. This book is one of a series of six penned under the title of "On the Table in 20 Minutes".

Cooking with feeling ~ Brenda

66

Tempting bite-sized beauties!

Miniature tart cases filled with a mild salmon curry, tender tandoori chicken skewers or mini meatballs – the start of a finger-food feast!

Cocktail-style parties featuring an elegant selection of finger food are becoming very popular. It can be very costly to have catered, however, as much of this style of food is labour-intensive to make. Cheaper offerings are usually limited to deep-fried snack food that has been mass-produced! Make your own, though, and you'll save money and enjoy the home-made flavours. The small pastry cases made in mini-muffin trays can be stored in an airtight container for up to one week. Then, with just a teaspoon or two of filling, you can make a quality snack that tastes fantastic! A well-made basic white sauce can become a mild curry sauce for prawns, chicken or salmon, or perhaps a mornay sauce for oysters and prawns, or even a parsley sauce for chicken. The secret to great finger or snack food is to plan well ahead of time and offer plenty of variety. Try to have your number of guests fairly fixed, so that you can prepare the right amount of food, leaving nobody hungry but also not creating extra work for yourself or too many leftovers.

Food has always inspired my imagination

various
vegetarian

various vegetarian

Hint: Vary the recipe by omitting the curry powder and stirring through finely chopped leg ham and a little wholegrain mustard. Delicious! White or wholemeal bread may also be used in this recipe.

Hint: Place the flour into a ziplock plastic bag with the mushrooms for easy, clean coating. This also works well with the crumbing mixture.

curried egg rolls

INGREDIENTS

6 hard-boiled eggs
small bunch chives, finely chopped
½ cup parsley, chopped
sea salt and freshly ground pepper to taste
1 teaspoon curry powder
½ cup mayonnaise
12 slices multigrain bread

Makes 12 rolls Calories 268
Fat 8g Preparation 8 mins
Cooking 8 mins

METHOD

1 In a glass bowl, mash the eggs well and add the chives, parsley, sea salt and pepper, curry powder and enough mayonnaise to bind the mixture.

2 Remove the crusts from the bread and lightly butter.

3 Spread some of the egg mixture on to each slice of buttered bread. Gently roll up and secure with a toothpick

crumbed button mushrooms

INGREDIENTS

20 button mushrooms
2 tablespoons plain flour
2 eggs, lightly beaten with a little milk
1 cup dried breadcrumbs
50g Parmesan cheese, grated
1 teaspoon oregano leaves
salt and pepper to taste
½ cup extra virgin olive oil

METHOD

1 Trim the stems of mushrooms to create a level base. Dust with plain flour. Coat the mushrooms with egg mixture. Combine the breadcrumbs, Parmesan cheese, oregano leaves and salt and pepper, and toss mushrooms in the mixture, thoroughly coating each one.

2 Gently fry mushrooms in extra virgin olive oil until golden turning a couple of times. Serve with sweet chilli sauce, aïoli, dijonnaise or your sauce of choice.

Makes 20 Calories 99 Fat 7g Preparation 12 mins Cooking 8 mins

crumbed button mushrooms

crumbed camembert wedges

Hint: The cheese wedges can be double-crumbed for extra crispness and protection for the delicate cheese.

INGREDIENTS

4 x 200g camembert cheeses

1 cup plain flour

3 eggs, lightly beaten with ½ cup milk

2 cups fine dry breadcrumbs

¾ cup olive oil

freshly ground black pepper and sea salt

cranberry sauce, to serve

METHOD

1 Cut each cheese into 6 wedges, and coat with the flour, egg and milk mixture and plenty of breadcrumbs.

2 Heat a frying pan to medium with a little oil. Fry the cheese wedges until golden. Don't overcrowd the pan and don't cover it. Cook for 2–3 minutes, turning a couple of times. Drain on a paper towel then keep warm in a low-heat oven. Serve with cranberry sauce on the side.

Serves 4 **Calories** 1420

Fat 103g **Preparation** 8 mins

Cooking 10 mins

crispy zucchini slices

INGREDIENTS

**3 large zucchini, cut into thick slices
on the diagonal
1 cup plain flour
2 eggs, beaten with ¼ cup milk
2 cups fine dry breadcrumbs
50g Parmesan cheese, grated
1 teaspoon dry thyme leaves
freshly ground pepper to taste
½ cup olive oil
sweet chilli sauce, to serve
light sour cream, to serve**

METHOD

1 Toss zucchini slices in flour, coat with the egg mixture and finally coat well with the combined breadcrumbs, Parmesan cheese, thyme leaves and ground black pepper.

2 Fry zucchini in olive oil over medium heat until golden. Serve with the light sour cream and sweet chilli sauce.

Hint: Do not overcook the zucchini slices, as they won't hold their shape and will become difficult to dip in the cream and sauce.

Makes 24 slices **Calories** 123
Fat 7g **Preparation** 6 mins
Cooking 8 mins

73

cocktail pumpkin and spinach pastries

cocktail pumpkin and spinach pastries

INGREDIENTS

1 bunch spinach or silverbeet

1 large onion, finely chopped

500g Kent pumpkin, peeled and chopped into 25mm cubes

2 large sebago potatoes, peeled and cut into 20mm cubes

salt and pepper to taste

1 cup parsley, chopped

½ teaspoon ground nutmeg

6 sheets butter puff pastry

METHOD

1 Preheat the oven to 200°C. Wash and finely chop the spinach, using the green part only.

2 Place the spinach, onion, pumpkin and potatoes into a large microwave casserole dish. Add 1 cup of boiling water and salt and pepper to taste. Microwave on high, covered, for 10 minutes.

3 Drain and mash the mixture. Add parsley and nutmeg, and cool the mixture.

4 Cut pastry into 9 squares for each sheet. Place a small amount of the mixture onto each square. Brush edges with milk to seal and fold to form a triangle. Bake for 8–10 minutes.

Makes 54 tiny parcels **Calories** 80
Fat 4g **Preparation** 12 mins
Cooking 20 mins

Hint: Refrigerate the mixture overnight to facilitate easy handling. Little pies can be made by using muffin trays.

the byron bay way

The idea for this recipe came from a vegetarian café in Byron Bay. In the 70s I took my sons, aged 6 and 12, for a holiday to this famous surfing mecca.

Perfect weather, stunning beaches and, – best of all, cheap – healthy, tasty food! Every glorious, sunny day was spent at the beach, with just enough tourists to make Byron Bay interesting.

What a great find was the tiny food store, which made the best pumpkin and spinach pastries! They were full of sweet pumpkin, mellow onion, steamed spinach and a hint of freshly ground nutmeg. Yum! Straight from a morning on the beach, the boys and I would head for our favourite food shop and our favourite dish.

Most people don't have the time or skill to make their own pastry, so I recommend using the pre-made variety.

various vegetarian

Hint: Lean ham, chopped capsicum or cooked prawns can also be added to the basic recipe.

Makes 16 **Calories** 52
Fat 4g **Preparation** 6 mins
Cooking 8 mins

mini *frittatas*

INGREDIENTS

6 free-range eggs
2 tablespoons cream
½ cup parsley, chopped
small bunch chives, chopped
4 button mushrooms, very finely chopped
50g Cheddar cheese, grated
salt and pepper to taste

METHOD

1 Combine all ingredients in a large bowl. Mix gently to combine all of the ingredients – do not over-beat, as the cooked mixture will toughen.

2 Heat a large electric frying pan on high and line with baking paper. Pour mixture onto the baking paper and reduce the heat to medium. Cover with frying pan lid and cook for 5–6 minutes until the frittata is just firm on top.

3 Cut into 4 equal pieces and carefully turn each piece. Cook for 2 minutes, then cut into small squares. Serve each in a paper case with a toothpick.

spicy cauliflower *flowerettes*

INGREDIENTS

3 tablespoons vegetable oil

3 cloves garlic, crushed

1 tablespoon curry powder

1 cauliflower, broken into small florets

½ cup water

salt and pepper to taste

METHOD

1 In a frying pan, heat the oil over medium heat and cook the garlic until just golden. Add the curry powder and cook for one minute.

2 Add the cauliflower and stir gently to coat. Add the water and salt and pepper to taste.

3 Cover and cook until the cauliflower is almost tender but not falling apart.

Hint: Serve with mini pappadums and natural yoghurt.

Serves 4 **Calories** 163
Fat 14g **Preparation** 5 mins
Cooking 12 mins

sweet potato and cummin cubes

sweet potato and cummin cubes

INGREDIENTS

2 teaspoons butter

⅓ cup olive oil

1 red onion, chopped

**500g sweet potato,
cut into bite-sized pieces**

2 teaspoons ground cummin

salt and pepper to taste

**1 cup fresh oregano leaves,
chopped**

METHOD

1 Heat the butter and oil in a frying pan, add the onion and cook until soft.

2 Add the sweet potato, cummin and salt and pepper to taste. Cover and cook until just tender. Add the oregano leaves and gently toss through the mixture.

Hint: Don't overcook the sweet potato cubes, as they will fall apart. Place a toothpick in each one to serve.

Makes 20 **Calories** 55 **Fat** 4g **Preparation** 5 mins **Cooking** 12 mins

79

various vegetarian

Hint: Add finely chopped lean double-smoked bacon to the mixture and cook with a couple of tablespoons of the mixture to serve as a light meal with a healthy salad. Top the meal-sized fritters with a little light sour cream and a sprinkle of fresh chopped chives. A light sprinkle of paprika can also be added.

Makes 12 **Calories** 137
Fat 9g **Preparation** 8 mins
Cooking 10 mins

zucchini fritters

INGREDIENTS

4 medium zucchini, grated
100g Cheddar cheese, grated
¾ cup self-raising flour
3 eggs
½ cup parsley, chopped
1 large brown onion, finely chopped
olive oil, for frying
salt and pepper to taste

METHOD

1 Combine all the ingredients in a large bowl and mix well.

2 Fry dessertspoons of the mixture in a small amount of olive oil over a medium heat, for 3–4 minutes each side.

80

seafood
selection

seafood selection

Hint: Remember that octopus has to be cooked either very fast or very slow to achieve tenderness. When buying seafood, it's a good idea to ask your fishmonger for a few hints on cooking it.

Hint: Try this recipe with strips of chicken breast fillet or green prawns, peeled and deveined.

barbecue baby octopus

INGREDIENTS

½ cup extra virgin olive oil

juice of ½ lemon

zest of 1 lemon

zest of 1 lime

2 tablespoons raw sugar

½ cup fresh oregano, chopped

salt and pepper to taste

2kg baby octopus

Makes 24 snack-sized portions

Calories 150 **Fat** 6g

Preparation 16 mins

Cooking 4 mins

METHOD

1 Combine the olive oil, lemon juice, lemon and lime zests, raw sugar, fresh oregano and salt and pepper to taste. Marinate the octopus in the mixture for 10 minutes

2 Preheat the barbecue on high, and cook octopus for 2 minutes each side.

3 Serve on a bed of mixed lettuce leaves with freshly ground pepper and sea salt and lime and lemon wedges.

thai fish bites

INGREDIENTS

500g firm white fish fillets, cut into bite-sized pieces

1 tablespoon Thai seasoning

2 tablespoons olive oil

1 teaspoon butter

½ cup coriander, freshly chopped

juice of 1 lime

salt and pepper to taste

METHOD

1 Coat the fish pieces with the Thai seasoning and fry over medium heat in the oil and butter. Do not overcook the fish – 2 minutes each side should be sufficient.

2 To serve, sprinkle the cooked fish bites with the chopped coriander, lime juice, and salt and pepper to taste.

Makes 10 **Calories** 88 **Fat** 5g **Preparation** 5 mins **Cooking** 4 mins

thai fish bites

seafood selection

Hint: Pacific oysters work well with these recipes. Fried shallots can be sourced from many Asian food stores.

An average natural oyster has 11 calories and 0.4g fat.

Serves 4 **Preparation** 4 mins

INGREDIENTS

4 oysters per guest
plus toppings of your choice

METHOD

1 Top each fresh oyster with a squeeze of lemon juice, a small piece of smoked trout, 1 teaspoon of light sour cream and a few chopped fresh chives. Salt and pepper to taste.

2 Top each fresh oyster with a couple of small fresh peeled prawns, teaspoon of mayonnaise, a hint of curry powder and a little finely chopped parsley. Salt and pepper to taste.

3 Top each fresh oyster with ½ teaspoon of red wine vinegar, finely chopped Roma tomato and finely chopped red onion. Salt and pepper to taste.

4 Top each fresh oyster with a squeeze of lime juice, a little pickled ginger, a few drops of tamari and fried shallots. Salt and pepper to taste.

pan-fried garlic prawns

INGREDIENTS

500g green prawns, peeled and deveined

4 cloves garlic, crushed

½ cup extra virgin olive oil

¼ cup lemon thyme leaves

1 teaspoon chilli flakes

freshly ground black pepper and sea salt to taste

METHOD

1 Combine all of the ingredients in a glass container with a cover. Allow to marinate for 15 minutes or more in the refrigerator.

2 Heat a frying pan, add the marinated prawns and stir-fry for 2–3 minutes or until cooked through. Don't overcook, as the prawns will become tough. Place a toothpick in each prawn and serve with lemon wedges.

Hint: The better quality the prawns, the better the result! To create a main course, simply add 1 punnet of cherry tomatoes during the cooking of the prawns and toss the mixture through cooked linguini.

Makes 12 **Calories** 122
Fat 10g **Preparation** 15 mins
Cooking 3 mins

85

salmon chats with dill cream

Hint: Place a small spoon in the dill cream to allow your guests to spoon it onto the salmon-wrapped chat potatoes. Horseradish cream can be used to replace the wasabi paste – use 2 teaspons or a little more of the horseradish cream.

INGREDIENTS

1kg small chat potatoes
200g smoked salmon, sliced
300mL light sour cream
1 tablespoon dill leaves, finely chopped
1 teaspoon wasabi paste
½ cup parsley, finely chopped
salt and pepper to taste

METHOD

1 Steam the chat potatoes until cooked but still firm, and allow to cool.

2 Wrap each chat potato in a small strip of smoked salmon and secure with a toothpick.

3 Combine the light sour cream, dill leaves, wasabi paste, parsley and salt and pepper to taste. Mix and serve in a bowl to accompany the salmon-wrapped chat potatoes.

Makes 12 **Calories** 133
Fat 6g **Preparation** 8 mins
Cooking 8 mins

sesame honey prawn sticks

INGREDIENTS

24 medium green prawns, peeled and deveined, leaving the tails intact

½ cup peanut oil

1 teaspoon sesame oil

freshly ground pepper and salt to taste

½ cup honey

1 tablespoon tamari

1 cup sesame seeds

50g iceberg lettuce, shredded

METHOD

1 Preheat the barbecue to high.

2 Thread one prawn on each of 24 pre-soaked wooden skewers. Brush with combined peanut oil and sesame oil and a little of the freshly ground pepper and salt, then cook for 1–3 minutes each side, subject to the size of the prawns.

3 Warm the honey and tamari in a microwave for 30 seconds on high. Dip the prawns in the honey mixture and then the sesame seeds. Serve on a bed of shredded iceberg lettuce.

Hint: Strips of chicken breast fillet can also be used for this recipe.

Makes 24 Calories 120
Fat 8g Preparation 10 mins
Cooking 5 mins

87

Hint: Try a variety of toppings – rare roast beef and horseradish, chicken breast (cooked and sliced), mayonnaise and double-smoked ham and honey mustard.

smoked salmon on garlic toast

INGREDIENTS

125g butter, softened

3 cloves garlic, crushed

1 cup parsley, finely chopped

3 crusty baguettes, cut into thick slices

200g smoked salmon, cut into bite-sized pieces

250g cream cheese

1 teaspoon lemon zest

salt and pepper to taste

1 large red onion, finely chopped

METHOD

1 Preheat the oven to 180°C.

2 Combine the butter, garlic and 1 tablespoon of the chopped parsley. Spread the mixture on one side only of each slice of baguette. Bake for 10 minutes, butter side up, then allow to cool.

3 Top each slice with a piece of smoked salmon, and a little cream cheese mixed with the lemon zest, salt and pepper, red onion and parsley.

Makes 24 **Calories** 110
Fat 8g **Preparation** 10 mins
Cooking 10 mins

fish bites

INGREDIENTS

500g firm white boneless fish, cut into 3cm cubes

½ cup plain flour

2 eggs, beaten with a little milk

1 cup fine dry breadcrumbs

1 teaspoon lemon pepper seasoning

¾ cup olive oil

lemon to serve

METHOD

1 Place fish cubes into a large ziplock plastic bag with the plain flour. Gently shake to coat each piece of fish.

2 Dip fish into the egg wash and then into the combined breadcrumbs and lemon pepper seasoning.

3 Fry crumbed fish pieces in olive oil on medium heat for 3–4 minutes until golden, turning a couple of times. Serve with wedges of lemon.

Hint: Always remember to undercook rather than overcook your fish, keeping the texture firm and the flesh moist and delicious.

Makes 10 **Calories** 287

Fat 20g **Preparation** 6 mins

Cooking 8 mins

Hint: Prawns, white fish or chicken can also be used in this recipe.

Makes 54 Calories 95
Fat 6g Preparation 5 mins
Cooking 15 mins

tiny salmon tarts

INGREDIENTS

6 sheets pre-made shortcrust pastry

1 tablespoon butter

1 tablespoon plain flour

1 teaspoon curry powder

1 cup milk, warmed

210g canned pink salmon, mashed with the liquid and bones

½ cup parsley, freshly chopped

juice of ½ lemon

salt and pepper to taste

METHOD

1 Preheat the oven to 200°C. Grease a small muffin tray.

2 Cut each sheet of shortcrust pastry into 9 equal round shapes. Press the round shapes into muffin cups and bake for 10 minutes.

3 Melt the butter in a small saucepan and stir in the plain flour and curry powder. Stirring constantly, add the milk and cook over a medium heat until the mixture thickens. Add the salmon, parsley, lemon juice and salt and pepper to taste.

4 Fill pastry cases with salmon mixture and serve warm.

chicken delight

chicken delight

Hint: Serve on a bed of shredded red and green cabbage and sprinkle with chopped shallots. Plenty of serviettes please!

Hint: Put a dollop of mayonnaise onto the final corner of the rolls to help them stick. Suggestions for other fillings include ham, mustard and grated cheese or smoked salmon, cream cheese and onion.

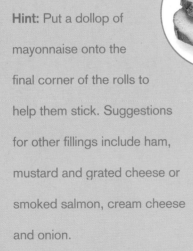

honey mustard chicken drumettes

INGREDIENTS

½ cup honey

¼ cup tamari

1 tablespoon German mustard

500g chicken drumettes

shallots, finely chopped, to garnish

METHOD

1 Combine the honey, tamari and mustard in a large microwave container. Heat for 30–50 seconds and stir to combine.

2 Toss the chicken drumettes in the honey mixture, making sure each one is well coated. Cover and cook for 10–12 minutes, stirring after 5 minutes. Garnish with shallots.

Makes 12 **Calories** 111

Fat 4g **Preparation** 2 mins

Cooking 12 mins

chicken and asparagus rolls

INGREDIENTS

20 slices buttered white bread, crusts removed

400g sliced chicken breast roll

400g canned asparagus spears, drained

3 tablespoons mayonnaise

salt and pepper to taste

METHOD

1 Place the pieces of bread between 2 pieces of baking paper, roll with a rolling pin until thin.

2 Place a slice of chicken and one spear of asparagus on to each slice of bread. Spread a tiny bit of mayonnaise on the chicken and asparagus, and season with salt and pepper.

3 Gently roll the bread on the diagonal to enclose the filling.

Makes 20 rolls **Calories** 140 **Fat** 7g **Preparation** 10 mins

chicken and asparagus rolls

chicken delight

Hint: After filling the celery bites, they can be topped with finely processed parsley. The mixture could also be put in a blender for a minute and then piped into the celery bite for a different presentation.

Makes 36 Calories 35
Fat 3g Preparation 10 mins

celery bites

INGREDIENTS

100g smoked chicken, finely chopped

1 red onion, very finely diced

250g cream cheese

1 teaspoon lemon zest

½ cup parsley, finely chopped

salt and pepper to taste

1 bunch celery, washed and cut into bite-sized pieces

METHOD

1 Combine all of the ingredients except for the celery pieces.

2 Fill the celery pieces with the mixture. Voila – tasty, healthy finger food!

chicken tandoori skewers

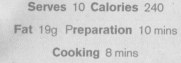

INGREDIENTS

500g chicken breast fillet, cut into long strips

½ cup olive oil

2 cloves garlic, crushed

salt and pepper to taste

300mL Greek-style natural yoghurt

2 tablespoons tandoori paste

2 teaspoons mint jelly

METHOD

1 Preheat the barbecue to high.

2 Thread the chicken on to pre-soaked skewers and brush with combined olive oil and garlic. Add salt and pepper to taste.

3 Combine 2 tablespoons of yoghurt with tandoori paste and brush on to the chicken.

4 Cook on the barbecue grill, and turn only once, after 3 minutes. Repeat the cooking time – allow an extra 2 minutes if the chicken is thick.

5 Combine the remaining yoghurt and mint jelly for a tasty dipping sauce.

Hint: Improve the flavour by marinating the chicken skewers for 2 hours or more.

Serves 10 **Calories** 240
Fat 19g **Preparation** 10 mins
Cooking 8 mins

smoked chicken and cucumber canapés

smoked chicken and cucumber canapés

INGREDIENTS

1 small tomato, quartered, seeds and liquid removed

salt and pepper to taste

250g cream cheese

100g smoked chicken breast, shredded

1 red onion, very finely chopped

1 tablespoon orange juice

salt and pepper to taste

2 large Lebanese cucumbers, cut into thick slices

METHOD

1 Cut the tomato pieces into small strips, then cut the strips into small cubes.

2 Combine all ingredients except the cucumber and the tomato.

3 Top the cucumber pieces with the chicken mixture and garnish with the little squares of tomato.

Makes 16 **Calories** 66 **Fat** 6g **Preparation** 15 mins

Hint: As an alternative topping for the cucumber canapés, combine the cream cheese with a 95g tin of tuna with lemon pepper.

elegant but healthy

Recently I attended an elegant cocktail party. During the evening, a range of fine wines and gourmet finger food was always on hand to tempt our tastebuds. It was a refreshing change to be offered such a diverse range of food that had been created with quality ingredients, and served in such an imaginative fashion.

The cucumber canapés were just one of many tasty treats on offer, and reminded me of the elegant cucumber sandwiches served at garden parties and high teas. A simple slice of cucumber can form the base for some delightful toppings, be they vegetarian or otherwise. Also, unlike crackers and breads, the cucumber will remain crisp and palatable over a longer period of time, making it ideal as an item to make ahead of time.

chicken delight

Hint: Serve crispy chicken fingers on a bed of steamed jasmine rice with sweet and sour sauce as a main course – include steamed seasonal vegetables.

Makes 10 fingers **Calories** 225
Fat 17g **Preparation** 10 mins
Cooking 6 mins

crispy chicken fingers

INGREDIENTS

500g chicken breast fillets, sliced into strips
½ cup plain flour
2 eggs, beaten
1 teaspoon cracked black pepper
sea salt to taste
½ cup peanut oil
1 teaspoon sesame oil
tamari, to serve
sweet chilli sauce, to serve

METHOD

1 Coat chicken strips with the plain flour and then dip into the beaten egg, seasoned to taste.

2 Heat the peanut oil and sesame oil over medium heat and fry the chicken strips until golden, turning a couple of times. Serve with tamari and sweet chilli sauce.

little chicken and mushroom pies

INGREDIENTS

500g chicken breast fillets, cut into small pieces

2 tablespoons butter

250g button mushrooms, finely chopped

2 tablespoons plain flour

½ cup milk, warmed

½ cup parsley, chopped

1 bunch fresh chives, chopped

salt and pepper to taste

6 sheets pre-made puff pastry

6 sheets pre-made shortcrust pastry

METHOD

1 Preheat the oven to 210°C.

2 Sauté the chicken in the butter until it changes colour then add the mushrooms and cook for a few minutes. Sprinkle the plain flour over the chicken and mushrooms and stir gently to combine.

3 Add the milk, parsley, chives and salt and pepper to taste. Stir until the mixture thickens. Allow to cool.

4 Line medium muffin trays with shortcrust pastry circles, spoon in the chicken mixture and top with puff pastry. Brush with a little milk, then bake for 10–12 minutes.

Hint: For variation, add 2 teaspoons of curry powder to the sauce when sautéing the mushrooms. Omit the chicken and add 1 large tin of red salmon, drained and mashed.

Makes 36 **Calories** 270 **Fat** 16g **Preparation** 5 mins **Cooking** 18 mins

cocktail chicken soy and linseed baskets

cocktail chicken soy and linseed baskets

INGREDIENTS

12 slices soy and linseed bread

olive oil spray

1 chicken breast, poached
and shredded

60g iceberg lettuce, shredded

2 tablespoons mayonnaise

METHOD

1 Preheat the oven to 180°C.

2 Remove the crusts from the bread and cut
each slice into circles with a pastry cutter. Roll
out each circle of bread between baking paper,
being careful not to break the bread.

3 Lightly spray muffin trays with olive oil and
press the thin circles of bread into each of the
muffin cups. Lightly spray each bread case
with the olive oil. Bake the bread cases for
10–12 minutes then allow to cool.

4 Combine the chicken, lettuce and
mayonnaise filling and put into the baskets just
before serving.

Hint: Meatballs and chutney or
many other tasty leftovers can
be combined to fill these handy
little baskets

Makes 12 **Calories** 171 **Fat** 7g **Preparation** 6 mins **Cooking** 12 mins

chicken delight

Hint: This mixture can be used in wontons or simply steamed for 8 minutes and served with soy sauce and chilli sauce, or combined with your home-made chicken broth for a tasty meal.

Makes 10 **Calories** 153
Fat 9g **Preparation** 8 mins
Cooking 10 mins

thai chicken meatballs

INGREDIENTS

500g chicken breast mince
1 bunch chives, finely chopped
2cm piece ginger, freshly grated
2 tablespoons coriander, freshly chopped
1 egg
½ cup multigrain breadcrumbs
2 teaspoons Thai seasoning
salt and pepper to taste
3 tablespoons cornflour
2 tablespoons peanut oil
1 teaspoon sesame oil

METHOD

1 Combine all ingredients except the cornflour, peanut oil and sesame oil.

2 Form into small meatballs, dust in the cornflour and cook in peanut and sesame oil for 3 minutes each side.

pork
and bacon

pork and bacon

Hint: Carefully separate the leaves of a pre-washed iceberg lettuce. Trim the outer edges of each leaf to create a lettuce cup for a piece of the pork. Chicken breast fillet can be used instead of pork in this recipe.

Hint: You can also make individual pies by using a large muffin tray and 1 egg per tart. Cook for 8–10 minutes.

chinese pork fillet

INGREDIENTS
2 teaspoons peanut oil
1 teaspoon sesame oil
500g pork fillet, trimmed of any sinew
1 clove garlic, crushed
½ cup hoisin sauce
1 tablespoon sweet chilli sauce
iceberg lettuce cups, to serve

METHOD
1 Heat the combined oils over medium heat in a frying pan. Add the pork and cook for 3–4 minutes each side. Add the hoi sin sauce and sweet chilli sauce. Cover, reduce the heat and simmer for 5 minutes.

2 Remove pork from the pan and allow to rest for 5 minutes.

3 Slice into bite-sized pieces and pour over the pan juices. Serve with lettuce cups.

Serves 8 **Calories** 88
Fat 3g **Preparation** 4 mins
Cooking 12 mins

egg and smoked bacon tarts

INGREDIENTS
2 sheets pre-made puff pastry
100g Cheddar cheese, grated
½ cup parsley, chopped
6 rashers lean smoked bacon
8 large eggs, 4 of them beaten
salt and pepper to taste
rocket to garnish

METHOD
1 Preheat the oven to 180°C.

2 Line 2 x 20cm quiche dishes with a sheet of puff pastry then sprinkle the bases with grated cheese and parsley.

3 Divide the bacon between the 2 dishes and add half o the beaten egg to each dish. Crack 2 eggs over each ta and season with salt and pepper.

4 Bake for 15–18 minutes. Cut in half to serve.

Serves 4 **Calories** 616 **Fat** 39g **Preparation** 10 mins **Cooking** 18 mins

egg and smoked bacon tarts

105

pork and bacon

Hint: To the basic vegetable mixture you could add cooked prawns, ham, salami, anchovies, olives, pineapple or any of your favourite pizza toppings. To achieve the best results, add the extra toppings after first marinating the vegetables.

Makes 24 wedges **Calories** 111
Fat 7g **Preparation** 10 mins
Cooking 10 mins

easy bacon pizza

INGREDIENTS

2 cloves garlic, crushed
1 red capsicum, finely sliced
1 large onion, finely sliced
200g button mushrooms, sliced
½ cup extra virgin olive oil
100g bacon, chopped
½ teaspoon chilli flakes
½ cup basil, chopped
1 large tomato, finely diced
6 small Lebanese flatbreads
50g Parmesan cheese, grated
100g Cheddar cheese, grated
sprinkle of oregano leaves
salt and pepper to taste

METHOD

1 Preheat the oven to 200°C.

2 Combine the garlic, capsicum, onion, mushrooms, olive oil, bacon, chilli flakes, basil and tomato in a covered container. Refrigerate for 10 minutes to marinate the vegetables.

3 Spray a little olive oil onto each Lebanese bread base. Top with marinated vegetables and sprinkle with the combined cheeses and oregano leaves. Season to taste. Bake for 8–10 minutes then serve hot from the oven.

italian tartlets

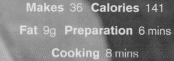

INGREDIENTS

4 sheets pre-made puff pastry

for each tartlet you will require

1 teaspoon tomato relish

2 small squares lean bacon, diced

½ small button mushroom, diced

2–3 cubes Cheddar cheese, diced

sprinkle of oregano leaves

salt and pepper to taste

METHOD

1 Preheat the oven to 200°C.

2 Using a scone-cutter, cut 9 circles from each sheet of pastry. Line the mini-muffin cups with rounds of pastry. Top with tomato relish, bacon, mushroom, cheese, oregano leaves and salt and pepper then bake for 8 minutes. Serve hot from the oven.

Hint: Use any ingredients used in traditional pizza and keep the quantities small.

Makes 36 **Calories** 141
Fat 9g **Preparation** 6 mins
Cooking 8 mins

pork and bacon

Hint: Don't over-fill, or the mixture will boil over and make the pastry soggy. The kids will love tartlets made with ham, pineapple and cheese.

marinated mix tartlets

INGREDIENTS

200g lean ham, finely chopped

2 cups mushrooms, finely chopped

½ cup olive oil

2 cloves garlic, crushed

1 red capsicum, finely chopped

1 onion, finely chopped

½ cup dried oregano leaves

4 sheets pre-made puff pastry

1 cup tomato and chilli pickle

150g Cheddar cheese, grated

METHOD

1 Preheat the oven to 200°C and grease muffin trays.

2 Combine the ham, mushrooms, oil, garlic, capsicum, onion and oregano leaves. Allow the mixture to stand for 5 minutes to infuse the flavours.

3 Using a scone-cutter, cut 6 circles from each sheet of pastry. Line muffin trays with the pastry circles and place 1 teaspoon of tomato and chilli pickle on each, then top with a little marinated mixture plus a small amount of grated cheese. Bake for 8 minutes.

Makes 36 **Calories** 127

Fat 9g **Preparation** 12 mins

Cooking 8 mins

pork and vegetable skewers

INGREDIENTS

2 red capsicums, cut into 3cm cubes

500g lean pork fillet, cut into 3cm cubes

36 button mushrooms

500g zucchini, cut into 3cm cubes

½ cup extra virgin olive oil

Moroccan-style seasoning

juice of 1 lime

1 bunch coriander, finely chopped

salt and pepper to taste

METHOD

1 Preheat the barbecue to high.

2 Thread the skewers, starting with the capsicum, then the pork, mushroom and finally the zucchini. Brush with the olive oil and dust generously with the Moroccan seasoning, then barbecue for 3–4 minutes each side.

3 Squeeze over the lime juice, add the coriander and sprinkle with salt and pepper to taste.

Hint: Prepare the skewers, in the morning for an evening barbecue, refrigerate until required. Experiment with different spice combinations, not using too large a quantity of any one in particular.

Makes 10 Calories 178
Fat 13g Preparation 12 mins

pork and bacon

Hint: The capsicum boats can be filled with the meat and rice mixture from the stuffed zucchini recipe on page 60.

Makes 24 **Calories** 45
Fat 3g **Preparation** 5 mins
Cooking 15 mins

stuffed capsicum boats

INGREDIENTS

3 small red capsicums
3 small green capsicums
250g lean bacon, finely chopped
1 onion, chopped
175g Cheddar cheese, grated
1 teaspoon chilli flakes
½ cup fresh basil, finely chopped
1 cup tomato paste
1 teaspoon fresh oregano leaves
salt and pepper to taste

METHOD

1 Preheat the oven to 180°C.

2 Cut each capsicum in half lengthwise and remove the seeds and white membrane.

3 Combine the bacon, onion, cheese, chilli flakes and the basil.

4 Fill each little boat with a small amount of tomato paste followed by the bacon and cheese mixture. Sprinkle with oregano leaves, and bake in a shallow baking dish for 15–20 minutes.

stuffed mushrooms

INGREDIENTS

200g bacon, chopped

100g Cheddar cheese, grated

1 bunch chives, chopped

1 tablespoon fresh oregano leaves, chopped

1 tablespoon dill leaves, chopped

½ red capsicum, finely diced

½ teaspoon chilli flakes

12 field mushrooms, stems removed

METHOD

1 Fry the bacon in a medium-sized frying pan for 3 minutes, stirring constantly.

2 Combine grated cheese, chives, oregano and dill leaves, capsicum, chilli flakes and the cooked bacon. Gently toss to mix through all the ingredients.

3 Place a heaped dessertspoon of mixture inside the mushroom where the stem has been removed. Microwave 6 mushrooms at a time for 1 minute on high or until the cheese melts.

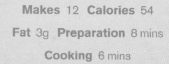

Hint: The stuffed mushrooms can be grilled for a couple of minutes instead, or barbecued until the cheese melts. Take care not to overcook them!

Makes 12 **Calories** 54
Fat 3g **Preparation** 8 mins
Cooking 6 mins

pork and bacon

Hint: Grated zucchini and carrot plus finely chopped parsley may be added for extra flavour, texture and nutritional value.

Makes 36 **Calories** 117

Fat 8g **Preparation** 15 mins

Cooking 15 mins

traditional sausage rolls

INGREDIENTS

500g sausage mince

200g bacon, chopped

1 egg

1 teaspoon dried mixed herbs

1 teaspoon oregano leaves, chopped

1 onion, very finely chopped

1 teaspoon salt

½ teaspoon ground black pepper

4 sheets pre-made puff pastry

milk, to glaze

METHOD

1 Preheat the oven to 200°C.

2 Thoroughly mix the sausage mince, bacon, egg, mixed herbs, oregano leaves, onion, salt and pepper together in a large bowl.

3 Cut each sheet of pastry into 3 equal strips.

4 Place a small amount of the mixture down the centre of each pastry strip. Fold the pastry over to enclose the filling, then cut each of the 12 filled strips into 3 equal pieces to create 36 sausage rolls. (You can freeze them at this point.)

5 Place the sausage roll, seam-side down, onto a baking tray lined with baking paper, glaze with milk and bake for 15 minutes. Bake a little longer if frozen.

lamb and beef

lamb and beef

Hint: Chicken tenderloins can also be used in this recipe. To make a yoghurt dipping sauce, combine freshly chopped mint and a little chutney with natural yoghurt.

Hint: To create a tasty meal, serve the Tuscan meatballs in a home-made tomato and garlic sauce. Serve over pasta of your choice. Divine!

curry yoghurt cutlets

INGREDIENTS

½ cup natural yoghurt
1cm piece ginger, grated
1 tablespoon lemon juice
2 cloves garlic, crushed
2 teaspoons curry powder
salt and pepper to taste
12 lean lamb cutlets
natural yoghurt to serve

Makes 12 Calories 90
Fat 5g Preparation 12 mins
Cooking 8 mins

METHOD

1 Preheat the barbecue to high.

2 Combine the yoghurt, ginger, lemon juice, garlic, curry powder and salt and pepper to taste. Marinate the lamb cutlets for 10 minutes.

3 Barbecue for 3–4 minutes each side, depending on the thickness of the cutlets. Serve with natural yoghurt.

tuscan meatballs

INGREDIENTS

500g beef mince
1 teaspoon dried rosemary leaves
½ cup chives, finely chopped
1 teaspoon lemon zest
1 egg
salt and pepper to taste
2 tablespons plain flour
½ cup extra virgin olive oil

METHOD

1 Combine all of the ingredients except the flour and oil. Mix very well and form into small meatballs using a dessertspoon. Roll the meatballs in the plain flour.

2 Heat the oil in a large frying pan over medium heat and fry the meatballs for 6 minutes, turning a few times.

Makes 10 Calories 188 Fat 15g Preparation 10 mins Cooking 6 mins

tuscan meatballs

lamb and beef

Hint: Other ingredients that would be suitable for this recipe include chunks of double-smoked ham, vintage Cheddar cheese, pickled baby onions, marinated mushrooms and cooked, diced chicken breast.

Makes 16 **Calories** 344
Fat 28g **Preparation** 5 mins

antipasto skewers

INGREDIENTS

1 teaspoon honey
1 tablespoon red wine vinegar
3 tablespoons extra virgin olive oil
leftover Tuscan meatballs (recipe page 52)
32 baby bocconcini cheeses
8 grape tomatoes, halved
16 pieces green capsicum
freshly ground black pepper and sea salt to taste

METHOD

1 Combine the honey, vinegar and olive oil in a small screw-top jar. Shake well and set aside.

2 Onto each of the small skewers, thread one of the bocconcini followed by a piece of tomato, another bocconcini, then a piece of capsicum. Finally thread on a Tuscan meatball. Follow the same order for each of the 16 skewers. Brush with a little of the dressing, season and serve on a bed of salad greens.

filo fingers with minced lamb

INGREDIENTS

1 large onion, chopped

2 teaspoons butter

500g lean lamb mince

2 tablespoons Madras curry paste

2 tablespoons tomato purée

salt and pepper to taste

12 sheets filo pastry

olive oil spray

METHOD

1 Preheat the oven to 200°C.

2 Fry the onion in the butter until starting to brown. Add the lamb mince and break up with a fork to prevent lumps forming. Cook for 5 minutes over high heat, then reduce the heat to medium.

3 Add the curry paste, stir and cook for 2 minutes, then add the tomato purée and salt and pepper to taste. Stir well to combine.

4 Lay 4 sheets of filo pastry out, spray each one with olive oil spray and top each with a second sheet. Spray again and top with a third. Cut each of the layered sheets into 3 equal strips, making 12 strips.

5 Spoon the lamb mixture onto the pastry and roll up to form a finger shape. Spray with extra olive oil and bake for 10–12 minutes.

Hint: Puff pastry triangles can be made using this tasty filling as well.

Makes 12 **Calories** 125
Fat 5g **Preparation** 12 mins
Cooking 15 mins

mini dillballs

mini dill balls

INGREDIENTS

kg very lean minced beef or veal
or a combination of both

1cm piece ginger, grated

1 bunch chives, freshly chopped

bunch fresh dill, finely chopped

1 egg

freshly ground salt and pepper
to taste

2 cups fine dry breadcrumbs

½ cup olive oil

METHOD

1 Combine all the ingredients except half of the dill and the breadcrumbs and olive oil. Mix well in a large bowl and form into small balls.

2 Roll the meatballs in the dry breadcrumbs and fry in the olive oil over medium heat, turning a few times, for 8–10 minutes until cooked through.

3 Serve with a wedges of lemon and garnish with reserved chopped dill.

Makes 24 **Calories** 143
Fat 8g **Preparation** 5 mins
Cooking 10 mins

int: These tasty cocktail meatballs freeze well, cooked or uncooked. A dill and caper
ayonnaise is the perfect dipping sauce when serving these little treats.

having a ball

By combining lean beef mince with finely chopped vegetables, you can create one of the most popular items of finger food. The secret to these tempting little morsels is to only use top-quality ingredients, finely chop the vegetables with a small food processor and include some fresh herbs that are also finely chopped. This will ensure the dill balls won't fall apart during the cooking process!

Meatballs can be found in most cuisines – just by including fresh ginger, fresh coriander and selected spices you can create Asian meatballs. These are fantastic if you also use chicken breast mince rather than beef mince. Italian meatballs should include the following ingredients – chopped basil leaves, crushed garlic and a little tomato paste.

When making the meatballs, I suggest you make a larger quantity than you require immediately, because you can freeze the uncooked meatballs for up to 2 months.

119

individual corn chip bake

Hint: There are many varieties of corn chips available. While it's worth experimenting with a few different flavours, traditional corn flavour is perhaps the best.

INGREDIENTS

250g chorizo sausage, sliced

100g packet corn chips

300g chunky tomato salsa

100g Cheddar cheese, grated

300mL light sour cream

1 avocado, peeled and mashed

½ teaspoon lemon pepper seasoning

juice of ½ lemon

½ cup fresh chives, chopped

salt and pepper to taste

METHOD

1 Preheat the oven to 200°C.

2 Quickly pan-fry the chorizo sausage pieces on each side and tip out onto absorbent paper towel.

3 Place corn chips onto a baking tray lined with baking paper. Top each corn chip with a teaspoon of salsa and a little grated cheese, then the sausage and a little extra cheese. Bake for 6–8 minutes or until corn chips are nice and crunchy and the cheese has melted.

4 Serve with the light sour cream and avocado mixed with the lemon pepper seasoning, lemon juice, chives and salt and pepper to taste.

Makes 24 **Calories** 127 **Fat** 10g **Preparation** 6 mins **Cooking** 8 mins

moroccan lamb meatballs

INGREDIENTS

500g lean lamb mince

1 teaspoon lemon zest

1 tablespoon Moroccan-style seasoning

1 medium brown onion, finely chopped

¾ cup parsley, finely chopped

1 egg

salt and pepper to taste

dry breadcrumbs to coat

½ cup olive oil

METHOD

1 Combine all of the ingredients except for the breadcrumbs and the olive oil. Mix well and form into small cocktail-sized meatballs, using a dessertspoon as a guide.

2 Roll the meatballs in the dry breadcrumbs and cook in the olive oil until golden, 3–4 minutes, turning a few times. Serve with a variety of dipping sauces.

Hint: Spice up the meatballs with the addition of 1 teaspoon of chilli flakes. Serve with a cooling yoghurt and mint dip.

Makes 12 **Calories** 191
Fat 13g **Preparation** 12 mins
Cooking 8 mins

121

lamb and beef

Hint: As an alternative, omit the curry powder. Instead, sprinkle with cheese and bake uncovered for 15 minutes.

Makes 24 **Calories** 68
Fat 3g **Preparation** 10 mins
Cooking 20 mins

stuffed zucchini

INGREDIENTS

1 large onion, very finely diced
2 cloves garlic, crushed
1 tablespoon olive oil
2 teaspoons curry powder
500g lean lamb mince
1½ cups long-grain rice, cooked
2 tablespoons tomato paste
salt and pepper to taste
½ cup water
2 tablespoons finely chopped mint
8 zucchini, cut into 6cm pieces
natural yoghurt, to serve

METHOD

1 Preheat the oven to 200°C.

2 Fry the onion and garlic in the oil, add the curry powder and cook for 1 minute.

3 Add the lamb mince and cook for 5 minutes, breaking it up with a fork to prevent large lumps forming. Add the cooked rice, tomato paste, salt and pepper to taste and ½ cup of water, and the mint. Stir to combine the mixture

4 Using a sharp vegetable knife, hollow each zucchini piece then fill with the lamb and rice mixture. Place in a shallow baking dish, cover with foil and bake for 15 minutes. Serve with natural yoghurt.

Brenda Kitchen's
CHILDREN'S MEALS
On the table
in 20 minutes

R&R PUBLICATIONS MARKETING PTY LTD

contents

introduction 126

brekkie dishes 129

chicken dishes 141

meat dishes 151

party snacks 163

sweet treats 173

Introduction
Children's meals

Look at food through the eyes of a child and discover the food they really love. It looks good, tastes great and suits their size.

I count myself lucky that, even from an early age, my boys loved their food. Like all children, they had their favourites. However, sugar-laden food and drinks weren't on offer. This meant that at meal times they were actually hungry! Portion size, colour, aroma and flavour all have a role to play in children's food. Food has to be fun and this requires parents to be creative and committed. There are always going to be fussy eaters, and finding food they like can be a challenge. Introducing new flavours from quite a young age is the best way to educate a child's palate. You'll be amazed at the foods that children love – don't be afraid of including strong flavours such as chilli, olives and even some curries.

I trust you receive as much enjoyment from using this book as I did when I created and wrote these easy recipes. This book is one of a series of six written by me under the title of "On the Table in 20 Minutes".

Cooking with feeling ~ Brenda

Food for kids is child's play!

Delight your children with the wonderful fresh food that is so readily available. Bursting with colour and flavour, all the food groups have much to offer.

Small meals with lots of colour and texture will appeal to children. The crunch of crispy crumbed food together with creamy mashed vegetables works well, for example. I believe that it's how we introduce our little ones to food that greatly influences their response. Often if we show dislike for a particular food, our children will follow.

Foods like raw peas, beans and carrots are a fantastic way to supplement healthy home-cooked foods. Grated vegetables can be easily added to favourites such as Bolognese sauce and meatballs. Mexican food was always very popular in our house: tacos, nachos and baked tortillas were consumed on a regular basis. With these dishes I would always add extra vegetables to the rich, spicy sauce to create a full-flavoured, healthy meal. Just like adults, children will eat well in a relaxed atmosphere. Remember also that children like to have their own special plates, cups and cutlery. Keep their meals small and appetising, with a little healthy treat to follow.

Food has always inspired my imagination

brekkie
dishes

brekkie dishes

Hint: The oregano leaves give a subtle pizza flavour to the muffin.

Hint: Use eggs at room temperature if possible and the mixture will remain soft. Cold eggs from the refrigerator can toughen the mixture.

baked bean muffin

INGREDIENTS

4 English muffins, halved
soft butter for spreading
420g canned salt-reduced baked beans
60g Cheddar cheese, grated
sprinkle of oregano leaves

Serves 4 **Calories** 292
Fat 8g **Preparation** 2 mins
Cooking 10 mins

METHOD

1 Preheat the grill. Toast the 8 English muffin halves and lightly butter each half.

2 Top with baked beans, about 1 tablespoon.

3 Lightly sprinkle each muffin with grated cheese and oregano leaves.

4 Grill until golden, and serve immediately.

cheesy scrambled eggs

INGREDIENTS

4 large free-range eggs
2 tablespoons milk
40g Cheddar cheese, grated
¼ cup parsley, finely chopped
salt and pepper to taste
2 teaspoons butter
hot buttered toast, to serve

METHOD

1 Lightly whisk the eggs and add the milk, cheese, parsley and salt and pepper to taste.

2 Heat the butter in a medium-sized non-stick frying pan until foaming. Pour the egg mixture into the pan and gently stir as the mixture thickens. When almost cooked turn the heat off and cover the pan with a lid.

3 Make the toast while the eggs are resting, then serve immediately.

Serves 4 **Calories** 240 **Fat** 14g **Preparation** 4 mins **Cooking** 10 mins

cheesy scrambled eggs

crunchy granola

Hint: This lovely natural cereal is packed with energy, so only a small serve is required. It's even great without milk as an after school nutritious snack.

Makes 10 portions
Calories 490 **Fat** 22g
Preparation 10 mins
Cooking 20 mins

INGREDIENTS

½ **cup honey**
½ **cup natural maple syrup**
4 **cups rolled oats**
1 **cup almonds, chopped roughly**
½ **cup walnuts, chopped roughly**
½ **cup sunflower seeds**
½ **cup pumpkin seeds**
1 **cup dried apricots, sultanas, cranberries and apple**
1 **teaspoon ground cinnamon**

METHOD

1 Preheat the oven to 180°C. Warm the honey and the maple syrup in a small saucepan.

2 Combine all of the remaining ingredients in a large bowl and mix through the warmed honey and maple syrup.

3 Spread mixture evenly onto a baking tray and bake for 15–20 minutes. During the cooking time, stir the mixture a little to make sure the nuts and seeds don't burn.

fluffy eggs

INGREDIENTS

4 large free-range eggs
1 tablespoon milk
40g Cheddar cheese, grated
2 slices ham, finely chopped

METHOD

1 Grease 8 non-stick egg rings. Lightly beat together the eggs, milk, cheese and ham.

2 Place the egg rings into a large non-stick frying pan over medium heat. Pour the mixture into each egg ring, being careful not to overfill them. Cover with a lid and cook until almost set. Gently turn each egg ring to complete the cooking of the fluffy eggs.

Hint: Line an electric frying pan with baking paper and cook the fluffy eggs on medium heat for a great result!

Serves 4 Calories 139
Fat 10g Preparation 2 mins
Cooking 8 mins

133

jeff's special poached eggs

jeff's special poached eggs

INGREDIENTS

4 large free-range eggs
hot buttered toast
Vegemite
salt and pepper to taste

Serves 4 **Calories** 205
Fat 9g **Preparation** 2 mins
Cooking 5 mins

METHOD

1 Grease 4 non-stick egg rings. Place a medium-sized frying pan over medium heat.

2 Put the egg rings into the pan and break one egg into each. Pour hot water into the pan to the level of the top of the egg rings. Bring the water to a simmer, lower the heat and cover. Cook until the eggs look a little firm and are opaque – for 3–5 minutes depending on how you like your eggs done.

3 Serve on hot buttered toast with a scrape of Vegemite and salt and pepper to taste.

back to basics!

Bryce, my 6-year-old grandson, is full of mischief, fun and always hungry – a real little dynamo. When I asked him to describe his favourite food, he promptly told me that it's the special eggs cooked by his dad!

My son Jeff is, in fact, a bit of a dab hand at cooking and did a fine job working with my company "Simply Cooking" over a number of years, often cooking in major shopping centres to promote food for specialty retailers. Jeff took to this like a duck to water – well done Jeff!

Basic cooking done really well requires skill and the desire to learn. Even cooking eggs well is something to master and be proud of. Be it a perfect boiled egg, poached egg, scrambled eggs, on omelette or the common fried egg, once you learn the basics you will have that knowledge for life. Jeff's method of cooking the eggs that Bryce loves is simple, clever and always gives a great result.

Hint: If you use a large frying pan, you can cook up to 8 eggs at a time.

Hint: Once cooked and cooled, the bread cases can be stored in an airtight container for a few days, or frozen to be filled later.

Serves 6 **Calories** 199
Fat 14g **Preparation** 10 mins
Cooking 16 mins

little bacon and egg tarts

INGREDIENTS

6 slices multigrain bread
1 tablespoon olive oil or soft butter
200g lean bacon, finely chopped
6 free-range eggs, lightly beaten
salt and pepper to taste

METHOD

1 Preheat the oven to 200°C and cut the bread into large circles.

2 Press the bread into a muffin tray and brush with the oil or butter. Bake for 6 minutes.

3 Sprinkle some bacon onto each of the bread cases, pour the egg mixture on top and add salt and pepper to taste. Bake for 10 minutes.

mighty mini muffins

INGREDIENTS

175g butter, melted

3 eggs, lightly beaten

¾ cup brown sugar

1 cup natural yoghurt

1 teaspoon bicarbonate of soda

1 apple, peeled and grated

1 cup carrot, grated

1 cup sultanas

¾ cup self-raising white flour

¾ cup self-raising wholemeal flour

½ cup rolled oats

METHOD

1 Preheat the oven to 180°C. Line a 24-muffin mini-muffin tray with cupcake papers.

2 Combine the melted butter, lightly beaten eggs and the sugar and mix well. Add the yoghurt and bicarbonate of soda. Gently mix together, add the apple, carrot and sultanas, and stir to combine. Fold through the flours and oats, but don't over-beat.

3 Place heaped teaspoons of the mixture into cupcake papers. Bake for 10–12 minutes.

Hint: Consider adding a small grated zucchini to the mixture for increased nutritional value, or even replacing the grated carrot with grated raw pumpkin.

Makes 24 Calories 164

Fat 7g Preparation 10 mins

Cooking 12 mins

sweetcorn and bacon fritters

INGREDIENTS

200g canned creamed corn
1 cup self-raising flour
2 eggs
40g Cheddar cheese, grated
½ cup parsley, finely chopped
2 rashers lean bacon, chopped

METHOD

1 Combine the corn, flour, eggs, cheese and parsley. Mix well and set aside.

2 Heat a non-stick frying pan over medium heat and fry the bacon until crisp, and stir through the corn mixture.

3 Fry tablespoons of the mixture in the frying pan used to cook the bacon. Once bubbles form on the fritters, turn them over and cook for 1–2 minutes. Serve with tomato or barbecue sauce.

Hint: Finely diced leg ham can be used to replace the bacon. Add the ham to the batter mixture and use a little olive oil to cook the fritters.

Makes 10 **Calories** 108 **Fat** 3g **Preparation** 5 mins **Cooking** 8 mins

yummy baked spaghetti

Hint: This recipe works well with a simple Bolognese sauce. Add cooked and puréed vegetables to the sauce mixture for added nutritional value.

Serves 4 Calories 479
Fat 19g Preparation 5 mins
Cooking 20 mins

INGREDIENTS

150g fast-cooking spaghetti
1 tablespoon olive oil
2 large onions, finely chopped
6 mushrooms, finely chopped
200g leg ham, finely chopped
700g bottled pasta sauce
120g Cheddar cheese, grated

METHOD

1 Preheat the oven to 200°C and grease the bottom of 4 ovenproof bowls.

2 Cook the spaghetti according to the directions on the packet, and stir through a little olive oil to prevent it sticking together.

3 Heat the olive oil in a non-stick frying pan over a medium heat, and gently fry the onions until soft. Add the mushrooms and cook for 3 minutes. Add the ham and pasta sauce, and stir to combine.

4 Layer the cooked spaghetti, sauce mixture and grated cheese in the ovenproof bowls. Repeat the process, ensuring you finish with the cheese on top, then bake for 10–12 minutes.

chicken dishes

chicken dishes

Hint: The chicken nibbles can be frozen once cooked and cooled. You can also serve them as a main course with salad or vegetables.

Hint: Cut the filled wrap in half for younger children. The mixture may also be served in an iceberg lettuce cup – just omit the shredded iceberg lettuce.

chicken nibbles

INGREDIENTS

500g lean chicken mince
2 teaspoons Moroccan seasoning
½ cup onion, very finely chopped
1 egg
1 medium carrot, peeled and finely chopped
1½ cups cornflake crumbs
2 teaspoons olive oil

Makes 10 **Calories** 112
Fat 6g **Preparation** 10 mins
Cooking 10 mins

METHOD

1 Combine the chicken mince, Moroccan seasoning, onion, egg and carrot in a bowl and mix well.

2 Form the mixture into small meatballs and roll in the cornflake crumbs.

3 Heat the oil in a frying pan over a medium heat. Fry the meatballs for 8–10 minutes.

4 Serve either hot or cold, with dipping sauces.

chicken and salad wrap

INGREDIENTS

1 cup cooked chicken
2 cups iceberg lettuce, shredded
2 tomatoes, finely chopped
1 cup carrot, grated
1 cup light cheese, grated
½ cup sultanas
mayonnaise to taste
salt and pepper to taste
4 pieces lavash or mountain bread

METHOD

1 Combine the chicken, lettuce, tomatoes, carrot, grated cheese, sultanas, mayonnaise and salt and pepper in a bowl, gently toss to combine.

2 Place 2 tablespoons of the mixture onto each piece of bread then roll to enclose the filling and serve immediately.

Serves 4 **Calories** 474 **Fat** 16g **Preparation** 15 mins **Cooking** 10 mins

chicken and salad wrap

chicken dishes

Hint: Other cooked and puréed vegetables, such as carrots, broccoli or pumpkin, can be used in this recipe.

chicken and noodles with green sauce

INGREDIENTS

2 cups noodles or pasta

1 tablespoon butter

500g chicken breast fillets, cut into bite-size pieces

1 onion, finely chopped

1 clove garlic, crushed

1 zucchini, grated

salt and pepper to taste

40g Cheddar cheese, grated

METHOD

1 Cook the noodles or pasta according to the directions on the packet. Heat the butter in a frying pan over a medium heat, and stir-fry the chicken for 5–6 minutes. Place in a low-heat oven to keep warm.

2 In the pan juices, cook the onion, garlic and zucchini until soft. Add the salt and pepper to taste. Purée the vegetable mixture and gently reheat.

3 Serve the chicken on top of the noodles with a little of the green sauce and grated cheese.

Serves 4 **Calories** 526

Fat 18g **Preparation** 10 mins

Cooking 16 mins

crisp chicken tortillas

INGREDIENTS

2 tablespoons olive oil

500g chicken breast fillets, cut into strips

½ cup plain flour

1 tablespoon burrito seasoning

2 eggs, lightly beaten

60g iceberg lettuce, shredded

4 tortillas

300g mild chunky tomato salsa

METHOD

1 Heat the oil in a medium-sized frying pan over a medium heat.

2 Dip the chicken strips in the combined plain flour and Burrito seasoning. Dip in the beaten egg and fry until golden, about 2–3 minutes each side.

3 Serve the crisp chicken, lettuce, tortillas and salsa separately to allow everyone to make their own tasty meal.

Hint: Accompany with light sour cream, grated cheese and avocado mashed with lemon juice to make a main meal.

Serves 4 **Calories** 463
Fat 24g **Preparation** 5 mins
Cooking 6 mins

Hint: Don't overcrowd the frying pan. Increase the heat in the pan if the chicken pieces are not browning quickly enough during the cooking time. This recipe also works well with firm, white, boneless fish pieces.

easy cheesy nuggets

INGREDIENTS

500g chicken breast fillets, cut into bite-sized pieces
1 tablespoon plain flour
1 tablespoon olive oil
1 egg, lightly beaten with a little milk
2 cups breadcrumbs
40g Cheddar cheese, grated

METHOD

1 Preheat an electric frying pan on medium heat.

2 Place the chicken into a large zip-lock bag with the flour. Seal the bag well and shake it to coat the chicken pieces.

3 Open the bag and add the egg mixture to the floured chicken. Hold the top of the bag firmly and mix the egg through the chicken by gently squeezing the bag.

4 Mix the breadcrumbs and the cheese, and add to the bag. Shake well to coat each chicken piece. Remove the chicken from the bag.

5 Heat the oil in the pan and cook the chicken pieces for 3 minutes each side or until golden.

Serves 4 **Calories** 532
Fat 22g **Preparation** 15 mins
Cooking 10 mins

easy chicken bake

INGREDIENTS

1 cup frozen baby peas

250g chicken mince

1 cup corn kernels, fresh or canned

juice of 1 lemon

salt and pepper to taste

3 cups cooked rice

80g Cheddar cheese, grated

METHOD

1 Preheat the oven to 180°C and grease 4 ramekins.

2 Cook the peas in a microwave oven according to the directions on the packet.

3 Combine the chicken mince, peas, corn, lemon juice and salt and pepper to taste.

4 Layer the rice, chicken mixture and the cheese, repeat the layers and bake for 15 minutes.

Hint: This simple recipe can also be made with cooked mini penne or any small pasta shapes.

Serves 4 **Calories** 410

Fat 13g **Preparation** 5 mins

Cooking 18 mins

Hint: Finely chopped leftover roast vegetables, lamb, beef or pork are great in this recipe.

Serves 4 **Calories** 328
Fat 17g **Preparation** 15 mins
Cooking 20 mins

mexican roll-ups

INGREDIENTS

2 cups cooked chicken
2 tablespoons light sour cream
300g mild chunky tomato salsa
1 cup button mushrooms, finely chopped
4 tortillas
60g Cheddar cheese, grated

METHOD

1 Preheat the oven to 200°C, and grease a shallow ovenproof dish.

2 Combine the chicken, sour cream, half the salsa and the mushrooms. Divide the mixture between the 4 tortilla and roll up to enclose the filling.

3 Place tortilla parcels seam side down in the baking dish. Spoon the remaining salsa over the tortillas and finally add the grated cheese. Bake for 15–20 minutes o until the cheese turns golden.

mini penne with chicken, cheese and tomato sauce

INGREDIENTS

1½ cups cooked chicken, cut into bite-sized pieces

400mL bottled pasta sauce

3 cups cooked mini penne or small pasta shapes

salt and pepper to taste

80g Cheddar cheese, grated

METHOD

1 Preheat the oven to 180°C and grease 4 remekins.

2 Combine the chicken, pasta sauce and penne, and add salt and pepper to taste. Divide between 4 ramekins. Top with a little grated cheese and bake for 10 minutes or until cheese is golden.

Hint: This recipe also works well with drained, canned tuna or cooked and chopped chicken sausages.

Serves 4 **Calories** 540
Fat 33g **Preparation** 10 mins
Cooking 10 mins

149

chicken dishes

Hint: Beef, pork or veal mince can be used in this recipe instead of the chicken.

Serves 4 **Calories** 129
Fat 8g **Preparation** 10 mins
Cooking 6 mins

rissole parmigiana

INGREDIENTS

500g chicken mince
1 egg
1 onion, finely chopped
1 teaspoon mixed herbs
salt and pepper to taste
1 tablespoon olive oil
300g chunky tomato salsa
60g light cheese, grated

METHOD

1 Combine the chicken mince, egg, onion, mixed herbs and salt and pepper in a bowl. Gently mix and form tablespoons of the mixture into small patties.

2 Heat the oil in a non-stick frying pan over a medium heat. Fry the patties for 3 minutes, pressing down with a fork to flatten them slightly. Turn the patties and spoon a little of the salsa onto the top of each patty. Sprinkle with a little of the cheese. Cover and cook for 3 minutes or until the cheese melts.

meat
dishes

meat dishes

Hint: As an accompaniment to the lamb sticks, consider serving a plate of raw vegetables cut into small pieces. These are often more appealing to small children than traditional salad or vegetables. Try slender strips of carrot, fresh raw green beans, fresh peas in the pod or even diced tomato.

Hint: Cut the sausages into bite-sized pieces before adding to the bean mixture. The corn chips can be used to scoop up the sausages and beans.

lamb sticks

INGREDIENTS

8 lean lamb chump chops, cut into bite-sized pieces
1 tablespoon olive oil
1 tablespoon Moroccan seasoning

METHOD

1 Thread the lamb pieces onto 4 wooden skewers, brush with a little olive oil, then sprinkle each one with a light dusting of Moroccan seasoning.

2 Pan-fry or barbecue for 3–4 minutes each side. Serve with tomato or barbecue sauce.

Serves 4 **Calories** 174
Fat 10g **Preparation** 15 mins
Cooking 8 mins

chipolatas, beans and corn chips

INGREDIENTS

500g beef chipolatas
1 onion, finely chopped
2 tomatoes, diced
410g canned baked beans
100g packet corn chips

METHOD

1 Heat a non-stick frying pan and dry-fry the chipolatas for 8–10 minutes, turning a few times. Remove from pan and fry the onion and the tomatoes in the same pan until soft. Add the baked beans and the sausages. Serve with the corn chips.

Serves 4 **Calories** 585 **Fat** 40g **Preparation** 5 mins **Cooking** 18 mins

chipolatas, beans and corn chips

home-made burgers

Hint: The burgers will not fall apart, even though there is no egg in the beef mince – the very lean mince and the high cooking temperature will keep the burgers together and give a lovely char-grilled flavour.

INGREDIENTS

500g very lean mince

1 large onion, finely chopped

2 teaspoons dried oregano leaves

salt and pepper to taste

4 flat hamburger buns, split in half lengthwise

100g iceberg lettuce, shredded

tomato sauce or barbecue sauce

3 firm tomatoes, sliced

METHOD

1 Form the mince into 4 patties.

2 Place 4 meatballs in a large non-stick frying pan over a medium heat. Top with a little onion, oregano leaves and salt and pepper to taste, and press onto the burger. Cook the burgers for 2–3 minutes on each side.

3 Toast the buns. Place lettuce, beef pattie, sauce, and tomato onto one half of a toasted bun. Top with the other half, and serve immediately.

Serves 4 **Calories** 370
Fat 11g **Preparation** 15 mins
Cooking 8 mins

154

cheesy meatballs

INGREDIENTS

1 carrot
2 sticks celery
4 mushrooms
½ cup fresh parsley
1 onion
500g lean beef mince
2 eggs
40g Cheddar cheese, grated
1½ cups fresh wholemeal breadcrumbs
½ teaspoon fresh thyme leaves, chopped
½ teaspoon fresh oregano leaves, chopped
salt and pepper to taste
400g canned chopped tomatoes

METHOD

1 Preheat the oven to 200°C.

2 In a food processor, finely process the carrot, celery, mushrooms, parsley and onion.

3 Combine the beef mince, eggs, grated cheese, breadcrumbs, thyme, oregano, the processed vegetables and salt and pepper in a large bowl. Form into meatballs the size of a walnut.

4 Heat a non-stick frying pan over a medium heat, and dry-fry for 5 minutes until brown. Place in a casserole dish and pour over the tomatoes, then cover and bake for 15 minutes. Serve with mashed potato, pasta or rice.

Hint: A small quantity of leftover roasted or steamed vegetables can be puréed and included in the meatball mixture for increased nutritional value.

Makes 20 **Calories** 77
Fat 3g **Preparation** 10 mins
Cooking 20 mins

155

meatballs with pasta

meatballs *with pasta*

INGREDIENTS

500g lean beef mince

¼ cup parsley, chopped

1 rasher bacon, finely chopped

1 tablespoon Parmesan cheese, grated

1 egg

1 small onion, finely chopped

salt and pepper to taste

700g bottled pasta sauce

3 cups cooked mini penne

METHOD

1 Combine the mince, parsley, bacon, Parmesan cheese, egg, onion and salt and pepper in a bowl, mix well and form dessertspoons of the mixture into small balls.

2 Heat a non-stick frying pan over medium heat and dry-fry meatballs for 6–8 minutes. Pour pasta sauce over the meatballs, cover and simmer very slowly for 10 minutes. Serve with the cooked mini penne or any small-sized cooked pasta.

Serves 4   Calories 676

Fat 13g   Preparation 10 mins

Cooking 18 mins

little fingers

Little people love little food! Instead of using the meatballs with the pasta, you can make baby burgers with the meatballs, small dinner rolls, a little salad and tomato sauce. Simply add the meatballs to a non-stick frying pan, then flatten each meatball by pressing down with a fork or egg slice. Cook over medium heat for 2 minutes each side and hey presto, tasty baby burgers!

Another great way to use the meatballs is to add them to a clear soup with noodles, cooking them briefly to produce a nutritious and flavoursome meal for tiny tots! Make plenty of meatballs and include a few in the school lunchbox as a great lunchtime treat! Or make a fun and colourful mixture by combining the meatballs with some crunchy celery and carrot sticks, cubes of cheese and cherry tomatoes.

Hint: Fresh herbs can be added to the sauce for a richer sauce. Try torn basil, flat-leaf parsley or torn oregano leaves.

Hint: Add grated vegetables to the basic meatloaf mixture to increase the nutritional value. A small amount of grated cheese can be used in the topping with the pineapple and bacon.

mini meatloaves

INGREDIENTS

500g lean beef mince

1 large onion, finely chopped

1 egg

1 teaspoon mixed herbs

salt and pepper to taste

225g canned pineapple pieces, drained

2 rashes lean bacon, finely chopped

METHOD

1 Preheat the oven to 200°C and grease 4 mini loaf pans.

2 Combine the mince, onion, egg, mixed herbs and salt and pepper in a bowl. Mix well and press the mixture into mini loaf pans. Top with the combined pineapple and bacon, then bake for 20 minutes.

Serves 4 Calories 278
Fat 11g Preparation 8 mins
Cooking 20 mins

pizza fingers

INGREDIENTS

4 slices Turkish bread, toasted
1 large tomatoes, finely chopped
2 slices ham, finely chopped
1 cup pineapple pieces, drained
80g low-fat cheese, grated

METHOD

1 Preheat the grill to high.

2 Spread a little of the tomato onto each slice of toasted Turkish bread, followed by the same amount of ham, pineapple and finally, the cheese. Grill until golden brown and cut into 12 fingers.

Hint: Small, wholemeal Lebanese flat breads work well with this recipe: cut into wedges to serve. Thinly sliced onion and mushrooms can also be used to enhance the flavour and nutritional value of the pizza fingers or wedges. Try cooked chicken or finely minced cooked lamb as an alternative to the ham.

Serves 4 **Calories** 171
Fat 3g **Preparation** 5 mins
Cooking 6 mins

pizza muffins

pizza muffins

INGREDIENTS

1 tablespoon olive oil
1 onion, finely chopped
1 clove garlic, crushed
150g lean leg ham, finely chopped
80g Cheddar cheese, grated
1 cup crushed pineapple
1½ cups plain flour
2 eggs, lightly beaten
2 teaspoons baking powder
75g butter, melted
1 teaspoon dried oregano leaves

METHOD

1 Preheat the oven to 180°C and grease a 12-muffin tray.

2 Heat oil in a non-stick frying pan, and gently fry the onion and garlic until soft. Add the ham and fry for 2 minutes. Cool the mixture and add to the remaining ingredients. Stir gently to combine – do not over-beat.

3 Three-quarter-fill each muffin cup, then bake for 20 minutes.

Hint: Once baked, the pizza muffins can be frozen for up to 2 months. Place a frozen muffin in a school lunchbox and it will thaw nicely in time for lunch.

Makes 12 **Calories** 191 **Fat** 11g **Preparation** 10 mins **Cooking** 20 mins

161

Hint: Make double the recipe and freeze the raw or cooked patties. They're great as a sandwich filling when cooked and served cold, or in a burger when hot.

pizza patties

INGREDIENTS

500g lean beef mince
½ cup crushed pineapple, drained
1 tablespoon tomato sauce
1 onion, finely chopped
½ cup cheese, grated
½ cup lean leg ham, chopped
1 egg
1 teaspoon dried oregano leaves

METHOD

1 Combine all of the ingredients and mix well. Form tablespoons of the mixture into patties.

2 Heat a frying pan, and dry-fry the patties on medium heat for 4 minutes each side. Serve hot or cold.

Serves 4 **Calories** 298
Fat 15g **Preparation** 10 mins
Cooking 8 mins

party
snacks

party snacks

Hint: A small amount of dip with the veggie sticks provides a great after-school snack.

Hint: Chicken sausages can be used in this recipe. A tablespoon of burrito seasoning mix can also be added to the sauce near to the end of the cooking time for extra spice.

dips and sticks

INGREDIENTS
250g light sour cream
250g corn relish
250g light cream cheese
95g canned tuna with lemon pepper
400g chunky mild tomato salsa
1 large carrot, peeled and cut into thin sticks
½ bunch celery, cut into thin sticks

Serves 4 **Calories** 313

Fat 16g **Preparation** 10 mins

METHOD

1 Combine the light sour cream and the corn relish, mix gently. Combine the light cream cheese with the tuna, and mix well. Serve mild chunky salsa straight from the jar. Serve 3 dips with the carrot and celery sticks.

little snags with yummy sauce

INGREDIENTS
500g chipolata sausages
1 onion, finely chopped
3 tomatoes, finely chopped
1 teaspoon sugar
salt and pepper to taste

Serves 4 **Calories** 387

Fat 32g **Preparation** 5 mins

Cooking 20 mins

METHOD

1 Dry-fry the sausages in a non-stick frying pan over medium heat for 10 minutes, turning a few times.

2 Add the onion, tomatoes, sugar and salt and pepper to taste. Lower the heat and cook, covered, for 10 minutes.

3 The sausages can be cut into bite-sized pieces once cooked or left whole. Spoon over the sauce and serve with hot buttered toast.

little snags with yummy sauce

Hint: Kids will have fun creating their own pizza – however, due to the heat of the oven, an adult should do the cooking. A sprinkle of chilli flakes and oregano leaves is great on these pizzas.

mini flatbread pizza

INGREDIENTS

4 mini wholemeal flatbreads

300g chunky tomato salsa

1 cup canned pineapple pieces, drained

2 slices leg ham, finely diced

40g Cheddar cheese, grated

METHOD

1 Preheat the oven to 220°C. Line 2 baking trays with baking paper.

2 Spread the flatbreads with about a tablespoon of salsa, a few pineapple pieces, a sprinkle of the leg ham and some of the grated cheese. Bake on the baking trays for 8–10 minutes.

Serves 4 **Calories** 123

Fat 3g **Preparation** 3 mins

Cooking 10 mins

nifty nachos

INGREDIENTS

150g packet plain corn chips

400g canned baked beans

300g mild chunky tomato salsa

80g Cheddar cheese, grated

1 cup light sour cream, to serve

METHOD

1 Preheat the oven to 200°C. Line a baking dish with baking paper.

2 Spread the corn chips evenly over the baking paper. Top with the baked beans, salsa and cheese. Bake for 15 minutes. Serve with light sour cream on the side.

Hint: Kids will love this simple, tasty dish. Cooked shredded chicken can be mixed with the salsa to replace the baked beans. Individual nachos can be made in a soup bowl and baked in the Preheated oven.

Serves 4 **Calories** 512
Fat 31g **Preparation** 2 mins
Cooking 15 mins

167

Hint: To always have some muffins on hand, double the quantities for this recipe, and store extra cooked muffins in the freezer for up to 2 months.

pineapple and carrot muffins

INGREDIENTS

1 cup plain wholemeal flour
1 cup plain white flour
½ cup sugar
1 teaspoon cinnamon
1½ teaspoons baking soda
pinch of salt
2 cups carrot, grated
3 large eggs, lightly beaten
2 tablespoons butter, melted
225g canned crushed pineapple

METHOD

1 Preheat the oven to 160°C and grease a 12-muffin tray.

2 Combine the flours, sugar, cinnamon, baking soda and salt in a large bowl. Mix together the carrot, eggs, melted butter and the crushed pineapple with the juice. Stir both mixtures together until just combined. Spoon the mixture into the muffin tray and bake for 15–20 minutes.

Makes 12 **Calories** 169
Fat 5g **Preparation** 5 mins
Cooking 20 mins

sausage and veggie rolls

INGREDIENTS

1 medium carrot, peeled
1 small zucchini
½ cup celery pieces
500g sausage mince
1 egg
1 teaspoon mixed dry herbs
salt and pepper to taste
2 sheets pre-made puff pastry
¼ cup milk

METHOD

1 Preheat the oven to 200°C. Line a baking tray with baking paper.

2 Finely process the vegetables and combine with the sausage mince, egg, herbs and salt and pepper to taste.

3 Cut each of the pastry sheets into 3 equal strips, and place some of the filling down the centre of each. Fold the pastry over to enclose the filling. Cut into 4 and place seam side down onto the baking tray. Brush with a little milk then bake until golden, about 15–18 minutes.

Hint: As these sausage rolls are intended for kids, they are smaller than the traditional sausage rolls from your bakery and, as a consequence, take less time to cook. Any vegetables of your choice can be used in the recipe. Reduce the meat and simply add what you like.

Makes 24 **Calories** 114
Fat 8g **Preparation** 10 mins
Cooking 18 mins

Hint: Place cooked croquettes in a warm oven while preparing the sauce.

sausage croquettes

INGREDIENTS

250g sausage mince
250g lean pork mince
1 large onion, finely chopped
1 egg
1 teaspoon rosemary leaves
salt and pepper to taste
1 cup dried breadcrumbs
3 tablespoons olive oil
4 medium tomatoes, diced
1 medium onion, chopped

METHOD

1 Combine the sausage mince, lean pork mince, onion, egg, rosemary leaves and salt and pepper, and mix well. Form tablespoons of the mixture into a sausage shape and roll in the dry breadcrumbs. Place the croquettes on a plate and refrigerate for 15 minutes to firm the mixture.

2 Heat the oil in a non-stick frying pan and fry the croquettes until golden 3–4 minutes each side.

3 To make the sauce, cook tomatoes and onion in a little olive oil, then blend to make a smooth, kid-friendly sauce. Serve with mashed potato.

Serves 4 **Calories** 559
Fat 35g **Preparation** 30 mins
Cooking 8 mins

tiny topless bolognese pies

INGREDIENTS

1 tablespoon vegetable oil

1 medium onion, finely chopped

250g beef mince

400g canned crushed tomatoes

1 teaspoon tomato paste

4 sheets pre-made puff pastry

120g Cheddar cheese, grated

METHOD

1 Preheat the oven to 190°C and grease a 12-muffin tray.

2 Heat the oil in a large, heavy-bottomed frying pan and fry the onion for 2 minutes. Add the mince and fry, stirring constantly to break up any clumps of meat, for 4 minutes, drain off any fat, then add the tomatoes and tomato paste. Stir the Bolognese occasionally until it starts to thicken, approximately 6 minutes.

3 Meanwhile, cut the pastry sheets into 9cm squares. Gently press pastry into the cups of the muffin tray and top each with a heaped tablespoon of warm bolognese sauce and a sprinkle of grated cheese. Bake for 10 minutes.

Hint: Combined ham, tomato and onion (finely chopped) can be used to replace the Bolognese sauce. Or add carrot, celery, mushrooms and zucchini to the Bolognese for extra nutritional value. The extra vegetables break down and become part of the thick, rich, red sauce.

Makes 12 **Calories** 301
Fat 19g **Preparation** 10 mins
Cooking 20 mins

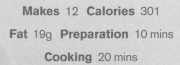

tuna and cheese rissoles

INGREDIENTS

4 large sebago potatoes, peeled and boiled until tender

1 onion, finely chopped

1 medium-size can tuna, drained and lightly mashed

1 tablespoon fresh parsley, chopped

60g Cheddar cheese, grated

1 egg

salt and pepper to taste

1 cup multigrain breadcrumbs

½ cup olive oil

METHOD

1 Place the cooked potatoes into a large bowl. Mash, and then add the onion, tuna, parsley, cheese, egg and salt and pepper, mix lightly to combine.

2 Refrigerate the mixture for approximately 10 minutes.

3 Form tablespoons of the mixture into patties and coat with the breadcrumbs. Heat the oil in a non-stick frying pan over a medium heat, and fry patties until golden, about 3–4 minutes each side. Serve with salad or seasonal vegetables.

Makes 8 **Calories** 330

Fat 21g **Preparation** 20 mins

Cooking 8 mins

sweet
treats

apricot balls

Hint: A few dates or some dried apple can be included in this recipe.

INGREDIENTS

zest of 1 orange
½ cup caster sugar
½ cup orange juice
1 cup dried apricots, finely chopped
1¾ cups desiccated coconut

Makes 24 Calories 72
Fat 4g Preparation 15 mins

METHOD

1 In a food processor, process the orange zest, sugar, juice, dried apricots and 1 cup of the coconut. Roll the mixture into small balls and roll in the remaining coconut. Store in the refrigerator or freezer.

Hint: If you're serving the muffins warm, they can be brushed with melted butter and sprinkled with cinnamon sugar.

apple muffins

INGREDIENTS

2 large eggs
¾ cup milk
4 tablespoons sugar
125g butter, melted
2 cups plain flour
1 tablespoon baking powder
1 large Granny Smith apple, peeled and grated
2 tablespoons icing sugar, for dusting

METHOD

1 Preheat the oven to 180°C. Grease a 12-muffin mini-muffin tray.

2 Beat the eggs, milk and sugar together in a mixing bowl. Add the butter and mix well. Sift the flour and baking powder, and gently fold into the wet ingredients. Stir through the grated apple, being sure not to over-mix. Place dessertspoons of the mixture into the muffin tray and bake for 12–15 minutes. Cool and dust with the icing sugar.

Makes 12 Calories 219 Fat 10.3g Preparation 5 mins Cooking 15 mins apple muffins

Hint: Place a couple of chocolate chips on top of each biscuit for a special treat.

Makes 24   Calories 103
Fat 5g   Preparation 8 mins
Cooking 15 mins

best bikkies

INGREDIENTS

100g butter
¼ cup golden syrup
½ teaspoon vanilla extract
½ cup sugar
1 cup rolled oats
½ cup desiccated coconut
1 cup plain flour
½ teaspoon baking soda
2 tablespoons warm water

METHOD

1 Preheat the oven to 180°C. Line a baking tray with baking paper.

2 Melt the butter in a large saucepan. Add the golden syrup and stir to combine. Add the vanilla, sugar, rolled oats, coconut and flour, then stir well.

3 Mix the baking soda and warm water together. Add to the mixture and combine. Roll the mixture into small ball place on the baking tray, and flatten the biscuits a little with a fork. Bake for 12–15 minutes.

chocolate cookies

INGREDIENTS

2 tablespoons butter, melted
¼ cup cocoa
1 cup sugar
2 large eggs, lightly beaten
pinch of salt
1 cup plain flour, sifted
1 teaspoon baking powder

METHOD

1 Preheat the oven to 180°C. Line a baking tray with baking paper.

2 Combine the melted butter, cocoa, sugar, eggs and salt in a bowl. Add the sifted flour and the baking powder. Stir well and place 12 spoonfuls of mixture onto the baking tray. Bake for 15–20 minutes.

Hint: Include cookies as a special treat in the school lunchbox, or serve as an after-school special snack.

Makes 12 **Calories** 151
Fat 4g **Preparation** 5 mins
Cooking 20 mins

muesli bars

muesli bars

INGREDIENTS

½ cup desiccated coconut
½ cup sesame seeds
1 cup rolled oats
½ cup sunflower seeds
1 cup sultanas
1 cup dried apricots,
finely chopped
¾ cup orange juice
1 cup dates, chopped
½ cup skim milk powder

Makes 12 Calories 221
Fat 9g Preparation 10 mins
Cooking 10 mins

METHOD

1 Preheat the oven to 180°C. Line a baking tray with baking paper and grease a 20cm cake pan.

2 Combine the coconut, sesame seeds, rolled oats and sunflower seeds and spread onto the baking tray. Bake for 10 minutes.

3 Combine the sultanas, apricots, orange juice and dates in a saucepan. Bring to the boil and simmer for 2 minutes. Cool the mixture and combine with the toasted mixture and skim milk powder. Press into the cake tin. Refrigerate for 24 hours before cutting into individual bars.

int: A little melted honey can be stirred through the oat mixture prior to baking to
ve added flavour and crunch! Bake this for a little longer.

aunty's treats

As a child, I loved when Aunty Jean came to stay with us at Clovelly. Nan and her dear friend would spend hours in our kitchen creating baking magic. Between the two of them they had many wonderful recipes.

The kitchen was a place where two close friends shared recipes, stories and secrets. The delicious aroma of baking wafted through our lives, too, making us feel special.

Marshmallow-topped caramel slice was one of Aunty Jean's specialities. I remember the caramel centre being made by boiling a can of condensed milk in our old copper for many hours. The end result was thick, gooey caramel – divine! To counteract all this sweetness, Nan created her crunchy and healthy muesli bars. We could have the caramel slice as a special treat, while the muesli bars were included in our school lunchbox.

However you look at it, my brother and I had the best of both worlds from two very special women who loved to bake.

fruit bubble slice

INGREDIENTS

125g butter
2 tablespoons honey
2 tablespoons sugar
3 cups Rice Bubbles®
½ cup sultanas

METHOD

1 Bring the butter, honey and sugar to the boil in a small saucepan, then simmer for 5 minutes.

2 Combine the Rice Bubbles® and sultanas in a large bowl. Pour the warm mixture over the Rice Bubbles® and gently stir. Pour into a cake tin lined with baking paper and refrigerate until firm, overnight if possible. Cut into squares for a tasty after-school treat.

Makes 12 **Calories** 152
Fat 9g **Preparation** 5 mins
Cooking 5 mins

mini fruit salad in an orange basket

INGREDIENTS

2 large oranges
1 banana
1 large Pink Lady apple
1 passionfruit
½ cup seedless grapes
1 cup natural yoghurt
2 teaspoons honey

Serves 4 Calories 157
Fat 2g Preparation 5 mins

METHOD

1 Cut the oranges in half and remove the flesh. Cut the orange flesh into small pieces.

2 Finely dice the banana and the unpeeled apple.

3 Combine the orange, passionfruit pulp, banana, apple and grapes. Mix gently and divide the mixture between the 4 orange halves.

4 Top with a little yoghurt mixed with the honey.

Hint: Depending on the time of the year, you may use other fruits in this recipe, such as kiwifruit, pears, strawberries, blackberries, blueberries or raspberries. These berries have great nutritional value. This recipe provides a great opportunity to introduce new fruits to your children in small quantities. You might also like to consider including a small quantity of dried fruits.

Hint: This healthy slice may be kept in the refrigerator for up to one week.

yoghurt muesli slice

INGREDIENTS

2 eggs, lightly beaten

3 tablespoons All-Bran®

500g natural yoghurt

2 cups toasted muesli

1 cup sultanas

METHOD

1 Preheat the oven to 190°C.Combine the lightly beaten eggs with all of the other ingredients and mix well.

2 Pour into a cake tin lined with baking paper and cook for 20 minutes. Allow to cool and then cut into squares.

Makes 12 **Calories** 171
Fat 5g **Preparation** 5 mins
Cooking 20 mins

Brenda Kitchen's

MARVELLOUS MELTS

On the table

in 20 minutes

R&R PUBLICATIONS MARKETING PTY LTD

contents

introduction 186

breakfast bounty 189

poultry perfection 201

hearty meat treats 211

fabulous fish 223

deli delights 233

Introduction
Marvelous melts

A mouth-watering melt is easy to prepare, and using quality fresh ingredients it can be very simple or gourmet. Beautiful, golden, melting cheese hot from the grill is a must for this tasty treat!

The basic melt has evolved into something quite spectacular from its humble beginnings. For many years, café menus were very limited in the melts that they offered. The best you could expect was ham, cheese and pineapple, or ham, cheese and tomato, or just cheese and tomato. In fact, my grandmother's home-made favourite was a combination of toasted thick white bread, real butter, thin slices of fresh pineapple and Cheddar cheese grilled to golden perfection.

These days there are an abundance of fabulous ingredients to choose from and you are limited only by your imagination. At home you can easily replicate the many combinations you enjoy in your favourite café. Be daring with the ingredients that you marry together: by doing this you could discover an exciting melt that could become a favourite healthy treat. Who would have thought that salmon, celery and cheese could taste so delicious when they come together in a melt?

I trust you receive as much enjoyment from using this book as I did when I created and wrote these easy recipes. This book is one of a series of six written by me under the title "On the Table in 20 Minutes".

Cooking with feeling ~ Brenda

Cheese lovers – get excited!

The melt was made for you! Bitey vintage Cheddar, creamy Brie, smooth Gruyère, fetta and many more wonderful cheeses will transform this simple fare.

Even something as basic as a melt can be delicious – it's very much determined by the quality of the ingredients. Compatible combinations can also greatly influence the end result. Let's talk about the bread that forms the base of all melts, too. We've come a long way from the burnt high-top loaf. This was the one that I picked up from our local bakery on the way home from school. Unsliced and warm from the oven, I remember it well!
Over time I've discovered a beautiful range of breads to delight the tastebuds – for example, there are the heavy, moist grain loaves, chewy malt loaves and even fragrant sourdough loaves. Many of these breads come from overseas cultures — I believe we are truly blessed to have this multicultural influence, as it brings with it a vast range of special ingredients that are well suited to melts. There are sensational cheeses, marinated vegetables, cured meats, seafood and poultry, in addition to the many styles of bread.

Food has always inspired my imagination

breakfast
bounty

breakfast bounty

Hint: The eggs can be fried in the normal way, but I find this version to be lower in fat and very tasty.

Hint: Omit the bacon for a vegetarian option. Slice the avocados close to cooking time to prevent discolouration.

bacon and egg melt

INGREDIENTS

8 eyes smoked lean bacon

4 large free-range eggs

4 English muffin halves, toasted

salt and pepper to taste

barbecue sauce

2 onions, peeled and finely sliced

4 slices low-fat Swiss cheese

Serves 4 Calories 507

Fat 25g Preparation 5 mins

Cooking 8 mins

METHOD

1 Preheat the grill on high.

2 Grill the bacon until crisp while the eggs are cooking.

3 Grease 4 egg rings and place them into a non-stick frying pan. Break one egg into each egg ring. Pour boiling water into the frying pan to the top of the egg rings. Simmer, covered, for 5 minutes.

4 Place one egg onto each of the toasted muffins, sprinkle with salt and pepper to taste. Top with 2 eyes of crisp bacon, barbecue sauce, onion and a slice of cheese.

5 Grill until golden and serve immediately.

bacon, avocado and cheese melt

INGREDIENTS

4 slices Turkish bread, toasted and lightly brushed with olive oil

2 avocados, peeled and thinly sliced

80g Cheddar cheese, grated

½ cup pickled onion, finely chopped

1 tablespoon finely chopped fresh thyme leaves

salt and pepper to taste

4 rashers bacon, finely chopped

METHOD

1 Preheat the grill on high.

2 Cover each piece of toasted Turkish bread with slices of avocado.

3 Combine the grated cheese, pickled onion, thyme leaves and salt and pepper to taste. Divide mixture between the avocado-topped toast and then sprinkle each one with chopped bacon.

4 Grill until the bacon becomes crisp and serve immediately.

Serves 4 Calories 660 Fat 38g Preparation 10 mins Cooking 6 mins

bacon, avocado and cheese melt

bacon, tomato and cheese melt

Hint: Mortadella or salami can be used to replace the bacon. Buy specialty breads such as sourdough, rye or Turkish, have them thick-sliced, and freeze until required. Make sure to keep each slice separate by using a few layers of cling film.

INGREDIENTS

4 slices Turkish bread, toasted and brushed with a little olive oil

4 vine-ripened tomatoes, sliced

salt and pepper to taste

200g smoked lean bacon, sautéed

2 tablespoons Parmesan cheese, grated

60g Mozzarella cheese, grated

1 teaspoon thyme leaves

METHOD

1 Preheat the grill on high.

2 Top each slice of Turkish bread with the tomato slices, salt and pepper to taste, chopped bacon, combined cheeses and the thyme leaves.

3 Grill until golden. Sprinkle with more pepper and serve immediately.

Serves 4 **Calories** 481
Fat 16g **Preparation** 4 mins
Cooking 6 mins

banana and pancetta melt

INGREDIENTS

8 slices pancetta

4 thick slices soy and linseed bread, toasted and brushed with olive oil

2 or 3 bananas, peeled and sliced

salt and pepper to taste

80g Cheddar cheese, grated

METHOD

1 Preheat the grill on high.

2 Grill the pancetta until crisp.

3 Cover each slice of toast with slices of banana, 2 slices of grilled pancetta, salt and pepper to taste and grated cheese.

4 Grill until golden and bubbling and serve immediately.

Hint: Streaky bacon can be used to replace the pancetta. Use bananas that are ripe but still firm. Slice the bananas close to the time of preparation to prevent discolouration.

Serves 4 **Calories** 301
Fat 11g **Preparation** 4 mins
Cooking 6 mins

193

crispy bacon melt

crispy bacon melt

INGREDIENTS

80g Cheddar cheese, grated

50g Parmesan cheese, grated

1 teaspoon dried oregano leaves

½ teaspoon ground paprika

salt and pepper to taste

4 slices pineapple, fresh or canned, drained well

4 slices heavy grain bread, toasted and lightly buttered

200g smoked bacon, finely chopped

METHOD

1 Preheat the grill on high.

2 Combine the Cheddar cheese, Parmesan cheese, oregano leaves, paprika and salt and pepper to taste. Toss gently to mix the ingredients together.

3 Place a slice of drained pineapple on each slice of toast. Divide the cheese mixture between the pineapple-topped toast and then sprinkle each one with the bacon pieces.

4 Grill until the bacon becomes crisp and serve immediately.

Serves 4 Calories 448

Fat 25g Preparation 6 mins

Cooking 4 mins

int: Slices of vine-ripened tomato can be used to replace the

neapple. Add freshly chopped parsley and chilli flakes to the cheese

ixture for extra flavour.

As a young girl, long before supermarkets were commonplace, I would pick up the weekly order from our local butcher shop. Amongst the variety of meats that my grandmother needed to create our tasty meals, there was always bacon. Nan often pan-fried it with diced onion and potato – this was one of our regular side dishes.

I am fortunate enough now to have a local butcher with a smokehouse, who sells the very best bacon and ham.

The wonderful smoky aroma greets you when you visit my special butcher shop. The unique depth of flavour of its lean bacon brings extra texture and taste to a crispy bacon melt.

Remember also that it is possible to freeze bacon simply by separating it into small portions, so you can always have this tasty ingredient on hand for your recipes.

Hint: Sprinkle the cheese with oregano leaves, paprika and black pepper to add extra flavour to the melt.

This recipe also works well with toasted Turkish bread: simple but very tasty!

ham and mushroom melt

INGREDIENTS

8 flat mushrooms, sliced

1 teaspoon olive oil

salt and pepper to taste

200g smoked leg ham slices

4 thick slices sourdough bread, toasted and brushed with olive oil

80g vintage Cheddar cheese, grated

METHOD

1 Preheat the grill on high.

2 Place the mushrooms in a small frying pan with the olive oil and sauté for 5 minutes. Add salt and pepper to taste. Drain off any liquid that is left.

3 Place the sliced ham onto each slice of toast. Top with sliced mushrooms and grated cheese. Grill until golden and serve immediately.

Serves 4 **Calories** 297

Fat 17g **Preparation** 4 mins

Cooking 5 mins

ham, cheese and tomato melt

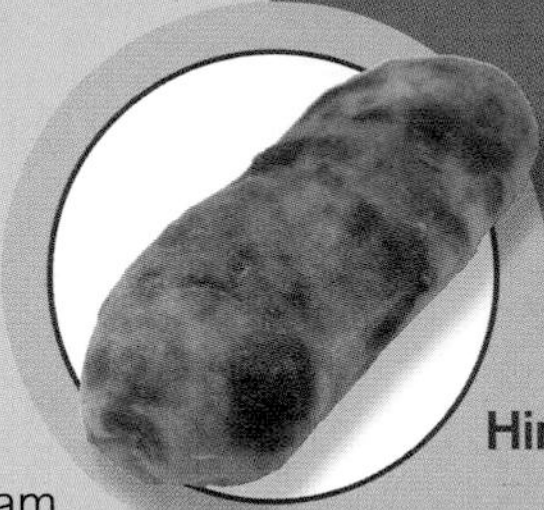

INGREDIENTS

4 slices Turkish bread, toasted and brushed with a little olive oil

200g sliced leg ham

4 truss tomatoes, thinly sliced

1 onion, peeled and thinly sliced

salt and pepper to taste

100g vintage Cheddar cheese slices

METHOD

1 Preheat the grill on high.

2 Top each slice of toasted Turkish bread with leg ham, sliced tomato, sliced onion, salt and pepper to taste and, finally, sliced vintage Cheddar cheese. Grill until golden and serve immediately.

Hint: Small pieces of leg ham can be purchased in most supermarkets. These can then be thick-sliced and used in this recipe to create a hearty snack or light meal. Vintage Cheddar cheese gives this everyday favourite a touch of gourmet flavour.

Serves 4 Calories 287
Fat 17g Preparation 3 mins
Cooking 4 mins

mexican stuffed bun

mexican stuffed bun

Hint: Add extra heat to the filling with chilli flakes or a little chilli sauce or paste.

INGREDIENTS

4 crusty white rolls

3 cups of chicken, cooked and diced

½ cup chunky tomato salsa

½ cup light sour cream

salt and pepper to taste

80g mature Cheddar cheese, grated

1 onion, finely chopped

½ cup corn chips, crushed

METHOD

1 Preheat the oven to 180°C.

2 Cut the top off each roll and hollow out to form a cavity for the filling.

3 Combine the chicken, salsa and sour cream in a bowl, mix gently to incorporate the ingredients, season and divide the mixture between the rolls and place on a baking tray.

4 Combine the cheese, onion and corn chips in a bowl, mix gently together. Top each roll with some of the mixture.

5 Bake for 15 minutes and serve immediately.

Serves 4   Calories 643   Fat 31g   Preparation 5 mins   Cooking 15 mins

breakfast bounty

Hint: This is a great way to use leftover meat from the barbecue – thinly sliced steak, for example. A good quality tomato relish can replace the barbecue sauce.

Serves 4 Calories 526
Fat 23g Preparation 6 mins
Cooking 12 mins

sausage *melt*

INGREDIENTS

8 thin gourmet sausages

4 long crusty white rolls, split lengthwise and toasted under the grill

barbecue sauce

2 onions, peeled and finely chopped

salt and pepper to taste

50g Cheddar cheese, grated

METHOD

1 Preheat the grill on high.

2 Dry-fry the sausages on medium heat in a non-stick frying pan for 4 minutes each side.

3 Place 2 sausages onto each roll, then top with barbecue sauce, onion, salt and pepper to taste and cheese. Grill until golden brown and serve immediately.

poultry
perfection

Hint: A mixture of corn kernels and creamed corn can be used in this recipe for added texture and flavour.

Hint: Slice thick slices of bread from a crusty loaf, rather than using the pre-sliced bread. Toast the bread well to prevent the topping soaking into the bread.

chicken and corn melt

INGREDIENTS

2 cups chicken, cooked and diced
1 cup creamed corn
1 bunch chives, finely chopped
salt and pepper to taste
4 slices of white bread, toasted and lightly buttered
40g mild cheese, grated
pinch of paprika

Serves 4 Calories 365
Fat 16g Preparation 5 mins
Cooking 5 mins

METHOD

1 Preheat the grill on high.

2 Combine the chicken, creamed corn, chives and salt and pepper to taste in a bowl, and mix gently. Divide mixture between the slices of toast. Top with some grated cheese.

3 Sprinkle with paprika, grill until golden and serve immediately.

chicken and asparagus melt

INGREDIENTS

1 bunch fresh asparagus
200g chicken breast fillet, cooked and diced
2 tablespoons finely chopped shallots
2 tablespoons egg mayonnaise
salt and pepper to taste
4 slices multigrain bread, toasted and lightly buttered
4 slices Swiss cheese

METHOD

1 Preheat the grill to high.

2 Trim the woody ends from the asparagus. Rinse in cold water and place in a covered, microwave-safe container. Cook on high for 1½ minutes.

3 Combine the chicken, shallots, mayonnaise and salt and pepper to taste in a bowl, and mix gently.

4 Divide the chicken mixture between the slices of toast. Top with a few asparagus spears and a slice of Swiss cheese. Grill until golden and serve immediately.

Serves 4 Calories 407 Fat 24g Preparation 5 mins Cooking 6 mins

chicken and asparagus melt

poultry perfection

Hint: Purchase the chicken from the deli or pan-fry strips of chicken breast fillet for 2–3 minutes each side on medium heat for a tasty home-cooked snack.

chicken and mushroom melt

INGREDIENTS

6 button mushrooms, thinly sliced

2 teaspoons butter

salt and pepper to taste

4 slices soy and linseed bread, toasted and lightly buttered

200g chicken breast fillet, thinly sliced and cooked

small bunch chives, finely chopped

4 slices Swiss cheese

METHOD

1 Preheat the grill on high.

2 Sauté the mushrooms in butter on medium heat until they start to soften, and season with salt and pepper to taste.

3 Top the toast with the chicken breast slices, mushrooms, chives and Swiss cheese. Grill until lightly golden and serve immediately.

Serves 4 **Calories** 361
Fat 19g **Preparation** 5 mins
Cooking 8 mins

chicken and spinach delight

INGREDIENTS

1 onion, peeled and finely chopped

2 cloves garlic, crushed

2 teaspoons butter

120g spinach or silverbeet, finely chopped

2 teaspoons plain flour

¾ cup milk

pinch of ground nutmeg

salt and pepper to taste

2 cups chicken, cooked and diced

2 large grain rolls, halved to form 4 bases

4 slices Jarlsberg cheese

METHOD

1 Preheat the grill on high.

2 Sauté the onion and the garlic with butter in a saucepan until soft.

3 Wash the spinach or silverbeet, leaving a little water on the leaves, then add them to the onion and garlic. Cover and cook for 5 minutes. Sprinkle the flour over the spinach mixture and stir well. Add the milk, nutmeg and salt and pepper to taste. Stir over medium heat to thicken, about 3 minutes. Add the chicken and stir well.

4 Divide the mixture between the 4 halves of grain rolls. Top with Jarlsberg cheese. Grill until golden and serve immediately.

Hint: Frozen spinach can be used in this recipe. The mixture can also be used in pastry triangles: bake at 200°C for 15–20 minutes.

Serves 4 **Calories** 385
Fat 19g **Preparation** 5 mins
Cooking 15 mins

205

poultry perfection

Hint: The cheeses can also be mixed through the chicken mixture and then divided between the pesto-topped toast before grilling!

chicken pesto melt

INGREDIENTS

1 small barbecue chicken, skin and bones discarded and meat roughly chopped

1 tablespoon tomato relish

salt and pepper to taste

4 thick slices wholemeal bread, toasted and lightly buttered

2 tablespoons basil pesto

80g Gruyère cheese, grated

50g Parmesan cheese, grated

METHOD

1 Preheat the grill on high.

2 Combine the chicken with the tomato relish, season with salt and pepper to taste, and mix gently.

3 Spread the toast with a little basil pesto and top with mixture and the combined cheeses. Grill until golden and serve immediately.

Serves 4 **Calories** 546
Fat 32g **Preparation** 5 mins
Cooking 5 mins

chicken swiss melt

INGREDIENTS

4 thick slices white bread, toasted and lightly buttered

200g chicken breast fillets, cooked and thinly sliced

1 tablespoon egg mayonnaise

½ teaspoon curry powder

1 red onion, thinly sliced

½ cup parsley, finely chopped

salt and pepper to taste

4 slices Swiss cheese

METHOD

1 Preheat the grill on high.

2 Cover each slice of toast with some of the sliced chicken breast and a thin spread of the mayonnaise mixed with the curry powder. Top with red onion slices, parsley, salt and pepper to taste and Swiss cheese slices. Grill until light golden and serve immediately.

Hint: This recipe works well with a crusty, high-top white loaf of bread. The ingredients in this recipe can also be used to make a traditional sandwich.

Serves 4 **Calories** 353
Fat 20g **Preparation** 6 mins
Cooking 5 mins

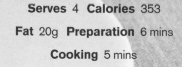

207

poultry
perfection

Hint: This chicken mixture can also be served on a bed of rice with an accompanying side salad.

Serves 4 Calories 328
Fat 21g Preparation 3 mins
Cooking 15 mins

mexican chicken melt

INGREDIENTS

2 teaspoons butter

1 clove garlic

200g chicken breast fillet strips

6 button mushrooms, finely chopped

salt and pepper to taste

1 tablespoon burrito seasoning

½ cup chunky tomato salsa

½ cup sour cream

4 tortillas

80g Cheddar cheese, grated

METHOD

1 Preheat either an oven to 200°C or the grill on high.

2 Melt the butter in a frying pan on medium heat and sauté the garlic, chicken strips, mushrooms and salt and pepper to taste for 5 minutes.

3 Add the burrito seasoning and cook for 1 minute. Stir in the salsa and sour cream.

4 Divide the mixture between the 4 tortillas and sprinkle each with cheese.

5 Bake on a baking tray or under the grill for 8 minutes and serve immediately.

turkey and special sauce melt

INGREDIENTS

1 tablespoon cranberry jelly

2 tablespoons apple sauce

2 teaspoons balsamic vinegar

2 tomatoes, finely chopped

1 onion, peeled and finely chopped

¾ cup parsley

salt and pepper to taste

200g sliced smoked turkey breast,

4 thick slices of grain bread,
toasted and lightly buttered

4 slices Cheddar cheese

METHOD

1 Preheat the grill on high.

2 Combine the cranberry jelly, apple sauce and balsamic vinegar and stir well.

3 Combine the tomatoes, onion, parsley, and salt and pepper to taste, and gently toss together.

4 Divide the smoked turkey slices between the toasted bread and top with the apple and cranberry sauce and the tomato, onion and parsley mixture. Finally, add the cheese. Grill until golden and serve immediately.

Hint: This recipe also works well with leg ham, sliced cooked pork or cooked chicken slices.

Serves 4 Calories 340

Fat 14g Preparation 6 mins

Cooking 5 mins

209

poultry perfection

Hint: Cooked chicken breast fillet (thinly sliced) can be used instead of turkey breast. Pesto can replace the green tomato relish.

Serves 4 **Calories** 486
Fat 33g **Preparation** 5 mins
Cooking 5 mins

turkey, brie and avocado melt

INGREDIENTS

1 ripe avocado, mashed with a little lemon juice and salt and pepper to taste
4 thick slices sourdough rye bread, toasted
200g turkey breast, thinly sliced
1 tablespoon green tomato relish
200g Brie cheese, sliced

METHOD

1 Preheat the grill on high.

2 Spread some of the avocado onto each slice of toast then top with quarter of the turkey breast, a thin spread o the green tomato relish and slices of Brie cheese.

3 Grill until melting and lightly golden and serve immediately.

hearty meat treats

hearty meat treats

Hint: Any vintage cheese can be used to replace the vintage Cheddar cheese. Mild German mustard can be used in place of the hot English mustard.

Hint: You can readily freeze portions of your favourite Bolognese sauce, then thaw and use it in this recipe.

balsamic beef melt

INGREDIENTS

2 teaspoons butter
4 thin slices scotch fillet steak
2 teaspoons balsamic vinegar
2 teaspoons brown sugar
2 onions, peeled and thinly sliced
4 slices Turkish bread, toasted
hot English mustard to taste
80g vintage Cheddar cheese, crumbled

Serves 4 Calories 288
Fat 12g Preparation 6 mins
Cooking 12 mins

METHOD

1 Preheat the grill on high.

2 Melt the butter in a frying pan over medium heat, add the steaks and cook for 2 minutes each side.

3 Add the balsamic vinegar and brown sugar. Stir to coat the steaks with the mixture. Add the onions and cook for a further 3 minutes uncovered.

4 Divide the steak and onions between the Turkish bread. Add a small amount of mustard then top with cheese. Grill until golden and serve immediately.

bolognese melt

INGREDIENTS

1 onion, peeled and finely chopped
2 cloves garlic, crushed
1 teaspoon butter
300g lean beef mince
1 tablespoon fresh flat-leaf parsley leaves
1 tablespoon fresh oregano leaves
1 cup tomato pasta sauce
salt and pepper to taste
4 English muffins, halved and toasted
80g Cheddar cheese, grated
50g Mozzarella cheese, grated

METHOD

1 Preheat the grill on high.

2 Sauté the onion and garlic in butter on medium heat for 2 minutes. Add the mince and fry for 4 minutes, breaking the mince up with a fork to eliminate lumps.

3 Add the herbs and pasta sauce, then season with salt and pepper to taste. Simmer for 10 minutes.

4 Divide the mixture between the 8 muffin halves. Top with the combined cheeses. Grill until golden brown and serve immediately.

Serves 4 Calories 416 Fat 17g Preparation 5 mins Cooking 20 mins

bolognese melt

italian flavours

Hint: Toasted crusty baguettes split lengthwise can also be used in this recipe. Cutting the baguette, once cooked, into manageable pieces can create finger food.

INGREDIENTS

½ cup semi-sun-dried tomatoes, finely chopped

½ cup black olives, sliced

½ cup chopped char-grilled capsicum

½ cup finely chopped basil leaves

salt and pepper to taste

4 foccacia, toasted

80g Mozzarella cheese, grated

50g Parmesan cheese, grated

1 teaspoon oregano leaves

METHOD

1 Preheat the grill on high.

2 Combine the semi-sun-dried tomatoes, olives, char-grilled capsicum, basil leaves and salt and pepper to taste in a bowl. Toss gently and divide between the 4 toasted foccacia.

3 Combine the cheeses and oregano in a bowl. Mix together and divide between the 4 foccacia.

4 Grill until the cheese bubbles and turns golden.

Serves 4 **Calories** 251
Fat 10g **Preparation** 8 mins
Cooking 6 mins

germanic *delight*

INGREDIENTS

4 thick slices heavy grain bread, toasted and lightly buttered

200g corned beef, cooked and sliced

1 cup sauerkraut, drained

1 teaspoon caraway seeds

4 gherkins, finely chopped

1 red onion, peeled and finely chopped

salt and pepper to taste

200g Brie cheese, sliced

METHOD

1 Preheat the grill on high.

2 Top each slice of toast with corned beef slices.

3 Combine the sauerkraut, caraway seeds, gherkins, onion, salt and pepper to taste. Top with slices of Brie cheese.

4 Grill until lightly golden and serve immediately.

Hint: A traditional German sourdough rye bread is also ideal for this recipe.

Serves 4 **Calories** 477

Fat 25g **Preparation** 4 mins

Cooking 5 mins

continental frankfurter special

continental frankfurter special

INGREDIENTS

4 crusty long rolls
4 continental frankfurters
1 tablespoon Dijon or German mustard
1 onion, finely chopped
4 gherkins, finely chopped
4 slices Jarlsberg cheese
salt and pepper to taste

METHOD

1 Preheat the grill on high.

2 Cut the rolls down the centre to create a space for the frankfurter. Place one frankfurter into each roll.

3 Top with a little mustard, onion and gherkin. Cut the cheese to fit the rolls and season with salt and pepper. Grill until golden and serve immediately.

Catrina, Wendy, Lorraine and I spent almost every weekend in summer at the beach. As school friends, we were a close-knit group. Our carefree days were filled with sunning our bodies, diving under the waves, looking at boys and lots of eating!

The takeaway food of choice was the humble hot dog, but not just any hot dog – the light crusty roll, tender continental frankfurt, mustard and tomato sauce was a stand-out. We could not stop at just one! As ravenous teenagers we loved the flavour of this truly special fast food.

As a weekend treat when I was growing up, my entire family would often have a casual meal of continental frankfurters and fried rice: a strange combination but a very good one!

Hint: Frankfurters are already cooked but can be heated briefly in boiling water. Once the water has boiled, add the frankfurters then turn off the heat and allow them to sit in the hot water for 5 minutes. Drain well before using.

hearty meat treats

Hint: This recipe works well as a pizza topping and is great for using small amounts of smoked meats.

Thinly sliced cabanossi, continental frankfurts, bacon or chorizo can be used.

meat lover's melt

INGREDIENTS

100g salami, finely chopped
100g pancetta, finely chopped
100g pastrami, finely chopped
½ cup black olives, sliced
2 firm tomatoes, finely chopped
1 cup flat-leaf parsley, finely chopped
2 teaspoons olive oil
salt and pepper to taste
4 thick slices crusty Italian bread, toasted
80g Mozzarella cheese, grated
50g Parmesan cheese, grated

METHOD

1 Preheat the grill on high.

2 Combine the chopped meats, olives, tomatoes, parsley, olive oil and salt and pepper to taste in a bowl, and toss gently. Divide the mixture between the toasted bread.

3 Combine the cheeses and sprinkle some over each piece of toast. Grill until golden and bubbling and serve immediately.

Serves 4 **Calories** 434
Fat 26g **Preparation** 6 mins
Cooking 6 mins

open burger melt

INGREDIENTS

200g lean mince, rolled into
4 equal-sized patties

1 large onion, finely chopped

salt and pepper to taste

4 flat hamburger rolls,
toasted and buttered

barbecue sauce

4 slices cooked beetroot

2 tomatoes, sliced

4 slices Swiss cheese

METHOD

1 Preheat the grill on high.

2 Flatten the beef patties and cook on high heat in a non-stick frying pan. Before turning, press some onion into the top of each one and season well. Cook for 3 minutes each side.

3 Place each burger onto a toasted bun. Top with barbecue sauce, beetroot slices, tomato slices and, finally, the cheese slices. Grill until golden brown and serve immediately.

Hint: Fried egg, bacon and pineapple can be added to this recipe to make a heartier meal.

Serves 4 **Calories** 370

Fat 15g **Preparation** 10 mins

Cooking 6 mins

219

steak and mushroom treat

INGREDIENTS

2 teaspoons butter

1 clove garlic, crushed

4 thin pieces scotch fillet steak

salt and pepper to taste

4 large flat mushrooms, thinly sliced

4 baguettes, halved lengthwise, toasted and lightly buttered

1 bunch chives, finely chopped

4 slices vintage Cheddar cheese

METHOD

1 Preheat the grill on high.

2 Heat the butter in a frying pan on medium heat and add garlic.

3 Fry the steaks in the garlic butter for 2 minutes each side and add salt and pepper to taste. Remove from the pan, add the mushrooms and sauté for 3 minutes.

4 Top each crusty baguette half with a piece of steak, some mushrooms and a sprinkle of chives. Add sauce of choice if desired, and top with cheese. Grill until the cheese is golden and serve immediately.

Hint: Thick slices of rare roast beef from the deli can be used to replace the steak. There is no need to cook the rare roast beef before assembling the melt.

Serves 4 Calories 406 Fat 18g Preparation 10 mins Cooking 8 mins

hearty meat treats

roast *pork delight*

Hint: Roast pork made at home is best for this recipe; slice it thinly for the best result.

Serves 4 **Calories** 302
Fat 13g **Preparation** 4 mins
Cooking 5 mins

INGREDIENTS

1 large onion, peeled and sliced

2 teaspoons butter

4 thick slices wholemeal bread, toasted

200g roast pork slices from the deli

½ cup apple sauce

salt and pepper to taste

4 slices Jarlsberg cheese

METHOD

1 Preheat the grill on high.

2 Sauté the onions in butter in a frying pan on medium heat until soft.

3 Place the toast onto a baking tray and top with slices of pork, apple sauce, onions, salt and pepper to taste and, lastly, the Jarlsberg cheese. Grill until golden and serve immediately.

fabulous fish

fabulous fish

Hint: Add char-grilled eggplant, capsicum or zucchini to this recipe to create a tasty vegetable meal.

Hint: This recipe can be used with tortillas and baked in a hot oven for 8 minutes. The mixture can also be used in a sandwich toaster if preferred.

olive and anchovy melt

INGREDIENTS

4 foccacia
¼ cup chunky tomato salsa
½ cup black olives, sliced
8 anchovy fillets, chopped
50g Mozzarella cheese, grated
50g Cheddar cheese, grated
50g Parmesan cheese, grated
½ teaspoon chilli flakes
½ cup basil leaves, finely chopped

Serves 4 Calories 266
Fat 13g Preparation 4 mins
Cooking 6 mins

METHOD

1 Preheat the grill on high.

2 Grill each foccacia lightly and spread each with a thin layer of salsa. Top each one with a sprinkle of olives and a few anchovy pieces.

3 Combine the cheeses, chilli flakes and basil leaves in a bowl and toss well. Divide the mixture between the 4 foccacia. Grill until golden and serve immediately.

prawn and pineapple melt

INGREDIENTS

3 cups small prawns, cooked, peeled and deveined
2 cups canned pineapple pieces, drained
4 long crusty bread rolls, halved lengthwise, grilled to a light golden colour
80g Cheddar cheese, grated
2 onions, peeled and finely chopped
2 cloves garlic, crushed
½ teaspoon chilli flakes
1 teaspoon dried oregano leaves
salt and pepper to taste

METHOD

1 Prcheat the grill on high.

2 Divide the prawns and pineapple between the open rolls.

3 Combine the cheese, onion, garlic, chilli flakes, oregano and salt and pepper to taste and spoon over the prawns and pineapple.

4 Grill until golden brown and bubbling and serve immediately.

Serves 4 Calories 498 Fat 11g Preparation 5 mins Cooking 5 mins

prawn and pineapple melt

lemon pepper tuna melt

Hint: For the best result, ensure the vegetables are very finely chopped. A can of pink or red salmon can be used to replace the tuna if you like.

INGREDIENTS

200g canned tuna in spring water, drained and flaked

1 teaspoon lemon pepper seasoning

1 bunch chives, finely chopped

½ cup semi-sun-dried tomatoes, finely chopped

½ cup finely chopped Lebanese cucumber

2 teaspoons lemon juice

2 teaspoons olive oil

4 thick slices crusty white bread, toasted

4 slices Swiss cheese

METHOD

1 Preheat the grill on high.

2 Combine the drained tuna, lemon pepper, chives, sem sun-dried tomatoes, cucumber, lemon juice and olive oil in a bowl. Toss gently to incorporate the ingredients well.

3 Divide the mixture between the slices of toasted bread Place a slice of cheese on top of each one. Grill until golden and serve immediately.

Serves 4 **Calories** 196
Fat 5g **Preparation** 8 mins
Cooking 6 mins

prawn mornay melt

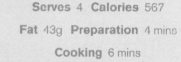

INGREDIENTS

2 cups small prawns, cooked, peeled and deveined

½ cup parsley, finely chopped

50g shallots, finely chopped

1 teaspoon Dijon mustard

¾ cup egg mayonnaise

1 tablespoon light sour cream

salt and pepper to taste

4 thick slices sourdough rye bread, toasted

80g Gruyère cheese, grated

METHOD

1 Preheat the grill on high.

2 Combine the prawns, parsley, shallots, Dijon mustard, egg mayonnaise, light sour cream and salt and pepper to taste in a bowl. Mix to combine the ingredients.

3 Divide the mixture between the slices of toasted rye bread on a baking tray and top with the grated cheese. Grill until a light golden brown and serve immediately.

Hint: The prawn mixture can be prepared a few hours ahead of time and placed in a covered container in the refrigerator – this will intensify all of the flavours.

Serves 4 Calories 567
Fat 43g Preparation 4 mins
Cooking 6 mins

227

salmon and celery melt

Hint: Canned tuna can be used in this melt: drain it before adding the other ingredients. Serving-sized pieces of Turkish bread can be frozen wrapped in a couple of layers of cling film to keep the slices separate.

INGREDIENTS

4 slices Turkish bread, toasted

2 teaspoons olive oil

210g canned red salmon, mashed with the juice and bones

2 stalks celery, finely sliced

1 tablespoon egg mayonnaise

2 tablespoons finely chopped fresh chives

salt and pepper to taste

2 tablespoons grated Parmesan cheese

50g Cheddar cheese, grated

METHOD

1 Preheat the grill on high.

2 Brush the toasted Turkish bread with olive oil.

3 Combine the salmon, celery, mayonnaise, chives and salt and pepper to taste in a bowl and mix. Divide the mixture between the toasted Turkish bread.

4 Mix the cheeses together and sprinkle on top of each salmon-topped Turkish bread. Grill until golden and serve immediately.

Serves 4 **Calories** 287
Fat 18g **Preparation** 4 mins
Cooking 5 mins

smoked trout melt

INGREDIENTS

200g smoked trout fillet, flaked

1 tablespoon sour cream

1 tablespoon egg mayonnaise

2 teaspoons horseradish cream

½ cup finely chopped shallots

salt and pepper to taste

4 thick slices sourdough rye bread, toasted and lightly buttered

4 slices Swiss cheese

METHOD

1 Preheat the grill on high.

2 Combine the smoked trout, sour cream, egg mayonnaise, horseradish cream, shallots and salt and pepper to taste. Mix gently.

3 Divide between the toasted rye bread then top with Swiss cheese. Grill until just melting and serve immediately.

Hint: Steamed Atlantic salmon can be used to replace the smoked trout. Finely chopped gherkins can also be added to the mixture for added flavour and texture.

Serves 4 **Calories** 334
Fat 19g **Preparation** 4 mins
Cooking 5 mins

sushi *flavours*

Hint: Swiss or Gruyère cheese also works well with this recipe. Look for the best-quality tuna in your supermarket and use the tuna in spring water for a good balance of flavours.

INGREDIENTS

200g canned tuna in spring water, drained and flaked

1 tablespoon dijonnaise

1 teaspoon wasabi paste

½ cup finely chopped shallots

1 Lebanese cucumber, finely chopped

salt and pepper to taste

4 slices sourdough bread, toasted and lightly buttered

4 slices mild Cheddar cheese

METHOD

1 Preheat the grill on high.

2 Combine the tuna, dijonnaise, wasabi paste, shallots, cucumber and salt and pepper to taste in a bowl. Mix gently.

3 Divide the mixture between the toasted bread slices. Top each one with a slice of cheese. Grill until light golden in colour and serve immediately.

Serves 4 **Calories** 296

Fat 15g **Preparation** 5 mins

Cooking 6 mins

tuna and chilli melt

INGREDIENTS

200g canned tuna in spring water, well drained

2 tablespoons shallots, finely chopped

1 teaspoon olive oil

1 red chilli, finely chopped

salt and pepper to taste

4 multigrain muffins, halved

1 avocado, mashed with a little lemon juice

60g Cheddar cheese, grated

METHOD

1 Preheat the grill on high. Combine the tuna, shallots, olive oil, chilli, salt and pepper to taste, and mix well.

2 Spread the toasted muffin halves with the mashed avocado. Top each one with the tuna mixture and finally the grated low-fat cheese. Grill until golden.

Hint: Try filling pre-cooked mini savoury tart shells with the tuna mixture, topping them with the low-fat grated cheese and baking them for 10 minutes at 180°C – truly tasty finger food for parties!

Serves 4 **Calories** 400
Fat 22g **Preparation** 5 mins
Cooking 6 mins

231

Hint: Look for the real Italian-style tuna in extra virgin olive oil. The quality of canned tuna varies greatly, so for best results, buy the very best!

tuna and mixed onion melt

INGREDIENTS

200g canned tuna in extra virgin olive oil

50g shallots, finely chopped

1 medium-sized red onion, finely chopped

½ teaspoon chilli flakes

½ cup Fetta cheese, crumbled

salt and pepper to taste

4 slices Turkish bread, toasted

80g Cheddar cheese, grated

METHOD

1 Preheat the grill on high.

2 Combine the tuna with olive oil, shallots, red onion, chilli flakes, fetta cheese and salt and pepper to taste in a bowl and toss gently.

3 Divide the mixture between the toasted Turkish bread and top with grated cheese. Grill until bubbling and golden and serve immediately.

Serves 4 **Calories** 401

Fat 27g **Preparation** 8 mins

Cooking 5 mins

deli
delights

deli delights

Hint: Spice up the cheese mixture by using hot salami to replace the ham. Add a little paprika, chilli flakes and dry rosemary leaves for an increased flavour boost!

Hint: This tasty mix can be used as a pizza topping or on Turkish bread.

pineapple and confetti cheese melt

INGREDIENTS
80g Cheddar cheese, grated
50g Parmesan cheese, grated
100g leg ham, finely chopped
1 red capsicum, finely chopped
1 bunch chives, finely chopped
4 slices Turkish bread, toasted and brushed with a little olive oil
4 thin slices pineapple, fresh or canned

Serves 4 Calories 323
Fat 18g Preparation 8 mins
Cooking 6 mins

METHOD
1 Preheat the grill on high.

2 To make the confetti cheese, combine the cheeses, ham, capsicum and chives in a bowl and mix well.

3 Top each slice of toasted Turkish bread with a slice of pineapple and a generous amount of the cheese mixture. Grill until golden and serve immediately.

cheese and garlic baguette

INGREDIENTS
2 cloves garlic
2 onions
2 teaspoons olive oil
½ teaspoon chilli flakes
50g Parmesan cheese, grated
80g Cheddar cheese, grated
1 teaspoon fresh oregano leaves
freshly ground black pepper
2 baguettes, halved lengthwise

METHOD
1 Preheat the grill on high.

2 Place the garlic, onion, olive oil and chilli flakes in a small food processor, and process until very finely chopped.

3 Combine the cheeses, oregano leaves and pepper. Spread the garlic and onion mixture evenly over the cut baguettes.

4 Divide the cheese mixture between the baguettes and place on a baking tray.

5 Grill until golden brown, then cut into serving-sized pieces and serve immediately.

Serves 4 Calories 264 Fat 14g Preparation 5 mins Cooking 6 mins

cheese and garlic baguette

Hint: This recipe makes good use of small quantities of meats and vegetables. Most supermarkets have a huge range of gourmet marinated and char-grilled vegetables that are ideal for this style of melt.

deli flavour melt

INGREDIENTS

200g mild salami, finely chopped

1 large red onion, peeled and finely chopped

¾ cup char-grilled capsicum, chopped

8 semi-sun-dried tomato halves, finely chopped

10 basil leaves, finely chopped, plus extra to garnish

1 tablespoon olive oil

salt and pepper to taste

4 thick slices crusty Italian-style bread, toasted

50g Parmesan cheese, grated

60g Cheddar cheese, grated

basil to serve

METHOD

1 Preheat the grill on high.

2 Combine the salami, onion, capsicum, semi-sun-dried tomatoes, basil leaves, olive oil and salt and pepper to taste. Toss gently and divide between the toasted bread. Top with the combined cheeses. Grill until golden and serve immediately.

3 Top with a few basil leaves.

Serves 4 **Calories** 479
Fat 34g **Preparation** 8 mins
Cooking 6 mins

pastrami and beetroot melt

INGREDIENTS

2 large onions, peeled and sliced

2 teaspoons butter

2 teaspoons brown sugar

2 teaspoons red wine vinegar

salt and pepper to taste

4 thick slices sourdough bread, toasted

200g beef pastrami, thinly sliced

8 slices canned beetroot, very well drained

4 slices Cheddar cheese

METHOD

1 Preheat the grill on high.

2 Pan-fry the onion in butter on medium heat for 5 minutes. Add the brown sugar, red wine vinegar and salt and pepper to taste, and cook for 3 minutes.

3 Top each slice of toast with slices of beef pastrami, sliced beetroot, onion mixture and cheese slices. Grill until golden and serve immediately.

Hint: Freshly cooked and sliced beetroot can be used in this recipe. Thick-sliced rye bread can be used to replace the sourdough bread.

Serves 4 **Calories** 305
Fat 13g **Preparation** 5 mins
Cooking 6 mins

paris best

238

paris best

INGREDIENTS

8 slices thick-cut white bread,
buttered on one side
4 thick slices leg ham
Dijon mustard to taste
4 slices Cheddar cheese
80g Gruyère cheese, grated
pinch of nutmeg
freshly ground black pepper

Serves 4 Calories 380
Fat 20g Preparation 3 mins
Cooking 5 mins

METHOD

1 Preheat the grill on high.

2 Lay 4 slices of bread onto a baking tray buttered side down. Top with ham, a thin spread of mustard and a slice of Cheddar cheese. Place a slice of bread on top of each sandwich, buttered side up.

3 Grill each side of the sandwiches until golden then top with Gruyère cheese, a little nutmeg and black pepper. Grill until melted and a light golden colour, then serve immediately.

the joys of travel

It is quite some years since I was in Paris, but I can still vividly recall the elegance, beauty and superb food of my favourite city. Paris is renowned for its food sense.

Real butter, freshly sliced lean leg ham, creamy cheese and thick slices of white bread are a must in this recipe – combined together they become a little bit of decadence to excite the tastebuds!

For me, food is all about "a little of everything you fancy" coupled with plenty of exercise. It works brilliantly and allows you to enjoy all the wonderful treats from all corners of the world.

As a typical tourist, I spent countless hours walking the wonderful avenues and the intricate lanes of Paris. My Paris Best toasted sandwich is the perfect food for tired tourists – simply satisfying, fresh and delicious!

Hint: Slices of lean leg ham can be used to replace the chicken breast fillet.

savoury chicken croissant

INGREDIENTS

4 fresh croissants

200g chicken breast fillets, cooked and sliced

4 thin slices pineapple

2 red onions, thinly sliced

4 slices Cheddar cheese

salt and pepper to taste

METHOD

1 Preheat the oven to 180°C.

2 Cut the croissants in half lengthwise and place the sliced chicken, pineapple, red onion, cheese and salt an pepper to taste into each one.

3 Place onto a baking tray and bake for 8–10 minutes.

Serves 4 **Calories** 503
Fat 28g **Preparation** 3 mins
Cooking 5 mins

tropical delight

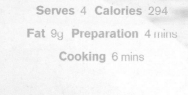

INGREDIENTS

3 rashers streaky bacon

1 cup canned pineapple pieces

3 bananas, sliced

sprinkle of cinnamon sugar

salt and pepper to taste

4 thick slices multigrain bread, toasted

4 slices Cheddar cheese

METHOD

1 Preheat the grill on high.

2 Grill the bacon until crisp.

3 Combine the pineapple pieces, banana slices, a little cinnamon sugar and salt and pepper to taste. Divide the mixture between the 4 pieces of toast and top with bacon and cheese. Grill until golden and serve immediately.

Hint: Flat hamburger rolls, split in half and toasted, can also be used for this recipe. Lean leg ham can replace the bacon.

Serves 4 Calories 294

Fat 9g Preparation 4 mins

Cooking 6 mins

turkey and cranberry melt

Hint: Smoked turkey breast can be used in this tasty melt. For a change of flavour and texture, use thick slices of sourdough rye bread and a mild Cheddar cheese.

INGREDIENTS

4 thick slices crusty bread, toasted and brushed with a little olive oil

200g cooked turkey breast, sliced

2 tablespoons cranberry sauce

½ char-grilled red capsicum, cut into thin strips

1 small red onion, finely sliced

80g Swiss cheese, grated

salt and pepper to taste

2 tablespoons olive oil

METHOD

1 Preheat the grill on high.

2 Top with turkey slices, cranberry sauce, char-grilled capsicum strips, red onion and some of the grated Swiss cheese, plus salt and pepper to taste.

3 Grill until golden and serve immediately.

Serves 4 **Calories** 394

Fat 24g **Preparation** 5 mins

Cooking 5 mins

Brenda Kitchen's
WONDERFUL WRAPS

On the table

in 20 minutes

R&R PUBLICATIONS MARKETING PTY LTD

contents

introduction   246

vegies and salad   249

poultry perfection   261

seafood selection   271

deli delight   283

hearty meats   293

Introduction
Wonderful wraps

Wraps have brought a whole new range of convenience food to busy people. With delectable fillings and wholesome breads, they are today's ultimate portable tasty food.

While holidaying in far north Queensland, my partner David and I visited the outstanding Mossman Gorge and spent two hours trekking through the amazing World Heritage – listed rainforest. The experience was stunning, exhausting and totally worthwhile. After all that exercise we were more than a little hungry. We made our way back to the township of Mossman to find somewhere to fuel our tired bodies. The café that we settled on was small, friendly and bursting with organic produce – "Goodies" by name. With healthy food and dedicated owners, we knew we were in for a treat! Wraps are an almost expected part of a health-conscious menu, as they often use wholegrains and fresh exotic ingredients. On this day in Mossman we selected wraps, of course, and they didn't disappoint.

I trust you receive as much enjoyment from using this book as I did when I created and wrote these easy recipes. This book is one of a series of six, penned under the title of "On the Table in 20 Minutes".

Cooking with feeling ~ Brenda

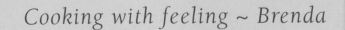

Wraps: wonderful, healthy fast food

Wraps have given the soggy sandwich the shove! It's easy to see why wraps have become the popular healthy option.

One of the reasons that I love to make wraps is the opportunity to stuff them with masses of healthy salad. You simply can't do that with the more common sandwich. A fantastic way to entertain on a sunny weekend is to have a wrap party – invite your friends to arrive around noon to enjoy a relaxed, casual lunch. The ingredients you can offer are endless and it's a real self-service affair! Firstly, select a range of wraps from the vast array now readily available. My favourite ingredients are hot, sliced roast lamb, creamy hummus, tabouli, fresh baby rocket, red onion slices, snowpea sprouts, lemon juice and a little good-quality olive oil to drizzle over the feast before enclosing it. Barbecues also work well with wraps – gourmet sausages are very popular and bring a new option to most weekend barbies. Usually burnt and not too healthy, the common sausage now has some real competition from the gourmet variety and is great in a wrap.

Food has always inspired my imagination

vegies and salad

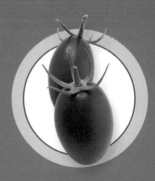

Hint: Green olives stuffed with anchovies, grated cheese and char-grilled eggplant are also wonderful in this recipe.

Hint: Cooked prawns, smoked turkey or cold barbecued chicken can be used in this recipe.

cheese and olive wrap

INGREDIENTS

1 cup black olives, sliced
16 baby bocconcini cheese
¾ cup semi-sun-dried tomatoes, chopped
3 cups rocket, roughly chopped
40g Parmesan cheese, grated
½ cup torn basil leaves
1 tablespoon olive oil
2 teaspoons lemon juice
salt and pepper to taste
4 lavash wraps

Serves 4 Calories 580
Fat 29g Preparation 5 mins

METHOD

1 Combine all of the ingredients, except the wraps. Toss gently and divide between the wraps. Roll each wrap to enclose the filling.

chicken caesar wrap

INGREDIENTS

4 rashers lean bacon, chopped
300g chicken breast fillets, sliced
2 teaspoons Moroccan-style seasoning
4 mountain bread wraps
1 teaspoon butter
80g baby cos lettuce, chopped
1 tablespoon caesar dressing
½ bunch chives, chopped
freshly ground black pepper
1 tablespoon olive oil

METHOD

1 Heat a frying pan and dry-fry the bacon on medium heat until crisp. Set aside to cool.

2 Sprinkle the chicken with the Moroccan-style seasoning. Cook the chicken in the combined olive oil and butter on medium heat for 3–4 minutes each side.

3 In a large bowl, combine the chicken, cos lettuce, bacon, caesar dressing, chives and black pepper. Toss gently and divide mixture between the 4 wraps. Roll each wrap to enclose the filling.

Serves 4 Calories 298 Fat 15g
Preparation 5 mins Cooking 15 mins

chicken caesar wrap

251

vegies and salad

Hint: To intensify the flavours of the vegetable mixture, cover and refrigerate for 30 minutes to 1 hour before use. You could also use the marinated vegetables on a pizza with a little cheese on top and pasta sauce on the base. Bake for 8–10 minutes at 210ºC.

Serves 4 **Calories** 154
Fat 6g **Preparation** 6 mins

marinated vegetable wrap

INGREDIENTS

200g button mushrooms, sliced
1 clove garlic, crushed
½ red capsicum, finely chopped
1 red onion, finely sliced
½ teaspoon dried chilli flakes
½ cup black olives, sliced
1 tablespoon extra virgin olive oil
2 teaspoons red wine vinegar
salt and pepper to taste
½ bunch coriander, finely chopped
60g spinach, stalks removed
4 mountain bread wraps

METHOD

1 Combine the mushrooms, garlic, capsicum, onion, chilli flakes, olives, olive oil and red wine vinegar in a glass bowl and add salt and pepper to taste. Stir gently.

2 Combine the coriander and spinach and divide between the wraps, then spoon on the vegetable mixture. Roll the wraps to enclose the filling.

niçoise wrap

INGREDIENTS

2 anchovy fillets
2 teaspoons olive oil
juice of 1 lemon
salt and pepper to taste
2 truss tomatoes, finely chopped
½ green capsicum, finely chopped
1 red onion, finely sliced
2 stalks celery, finely chopped
½ cup black olives, sliced
½ cup parsley, finely chopped
200g canned tuna in extra virgin olive oil
2 hard-boiled eggs, peeled and chopped
4 lavash wraps

METHOD

1 Mash the anchovies with the olive oil, lemon juice and salt and pepper to taste.

2 Combine the tomatoes, capsicum, red onion, celery, olives and parsley in a bowl and toss gently. Add the dressing, tuna with oil, and the hard-boiled eggs and toss gently.

3 Divide the salad between the wraps and roll each wrap to enclose the filling.

Hint: For a gourmet touch to this recipe, cook fresh tuna instead of using the canned variety.

Serves 4 **Calories** 415
Fat 16g **Preparation** 10 mins

raw energy wrap

raw energy wrap

INGREDIENTS

1 large carrot, peeled and grated

1 red onion, finely chopped

1 raw beetroot, peeled and grated

1 cup snowpea sprouts

green capsicum, finely chopped

2 truss tomatoes, finely chopped

1 cup sultanas

1 cup crushed peanuts

juice of 1 lemon

2 teaspoons honey, warmed in a microwave oven for 15 seconds

1 tablespoon extra virgin olive oil

salt and pepper to taste

4 wholemeal lavash wraps

Serves 4 **Calories** 632
Fat 23g **Preparation** 12 mins

METHOD

1 In a large bowl, combine the salad ingredients, sultanas, peanuts, lemon juice, honey, extra virgin olive oil and salt and pepper to taste. Toss gently and divide between the 4 wraps. Roll each wrap to enclose the filling.

int: To add extra protein to this recipe you could include fine strips of sashimi-grade
na, slivered almonds or avocado slices.

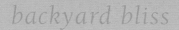

backyard bliss

Our suburban backyard was a sea of wonderful fresh vegetables: everything from ripe red tomatoes, beans, beetroot, spinach and sweetcorn, through to fragrant lettuce with an aroma like freshly cut grass. My grandmother turned the fresh produce into memorable meals every day of the week. At our seaside home, Nan created tasty food for all seasons: big, robust dishes in the cooler months and fantastic salads for summer. Nan was way ahead of her time when it came to being inventive with food! Most families would be familiar with beetroot in a can that stained everything it touched. Well, Nan made a beetroot salad using the raw grated vegetable, flavoured with malt vinegar and a little sugar, salt and pepper. This great-tasting salad was full of rich earthy flavours and goodness. Some years later I found it being used as an ingredient in vegetarian burgers in health cafés!

smoked ham *and parsley salad wrap*

Hint: Red wine vinegar can be used to replace the balsamic vinegar. Pastrami or mortadella can replace the smoked ham.

Serves 4 **Calories** 374

Fat 9g **Preparation** 6 mins

INGREDIENTS

1½ **cups parsley, finely chopped**
2 **truss tomatoes, finely diced**
1 **large red onion, finely diced**
3 **teaspoons extra virgin olive oil**
2 **teaspoons balsamic vinegar**
4 **Lebanese flatbread wraps**
2 **tablespoons hummus**
200g **lean smoked ham**
80g **Mesclun leaves**
salt and pepper to taste

METHOD

1 Combine the parsley, tomatoes, onion, extra virgin olive oil and balsamic vinegar in a bowl and stir gently to mix the ingredients well.

2 Spread each wrap with a little hummus and top with the slices of smoked ham.

3 Divide the parsley salad and Mesclun leaves between the wraps. Add salt and pepper to taste. Roll the wrap to enclose the filling.

sticky tofu wrap

INGREDIENTS

350g firm tofu, cubed
1 tablespoon olive oil
2 tablespoons tamari
1 cup apple juice
1cm piece ginger, grated
1 teaspoon lemon juice
1 carrot, peeled and grated
2 shallots, finely chopped
1 cup bean sprouts
80g iceberg lettuce, shredded
1 cup Thai basil leaves, chopped
4 mountain bread wraps

METHOD

1 Fry the tofu in olive oil for 10 minutes or until brown. Marinate the cooked tofu in the tamari, apple juice, ginger and lemon juice for 5 minutes.

2 Preheat the oven to 210°C. Bake the tofu for 5 minutes and combine with the salad ingredients, then toss gently. Divide the mixture between the wraps and roll each wrap to enclose the filling.

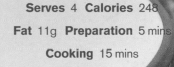

Hint: To shorten the preparation time, consider simmering the tofu in a teriyaki marinade from the supermarket. Use 2 tablespoons of marinade and simmer for 8 minutes, then don't bake the tofu!

Serves 4 **Calories** 248
Fat 11g **Preparation** 5 mins
Cooking 15 mins

257

sesame burger wrap

sesame burger wrap

INGREDIENTS

Burgers
1 cup sesame seeds
1 cup plain wholemeal flour
2 carrot, grated
1 large onion, finely sliced
1 cup parsley, finely chopped
½ cup basil, finely chopped
¼ cup tamari
1 tablespoon extra virgin olive oil

Salad
4 cups mixed salad leaves
2 tomatoes, finely chopped
1 Lebanese cucumber, finely chopped
juice of 1 lemon
1 tablespoon extra virgin olive oil
4 wholemeal wraps
sauce of your choice

METHOD

1 Combine the salad ingredients in a bowl and toss gently together.

2 To make the burgers, combine the burger ingredients except for the oil, and add enough water to make a thick batter consistency. Heat the oil in a frying pan over a high heat. Place tablespoons of mixture in the pan, flatten and cook for 4–5 minutes each side until golden. Remove the burgers from the pan and cut them in half to fit the wrap.

3 Divide the salad between the wraps and top with the burgers and the sauce of your choice. Roll each wrap to enclose the filling and serve immediately.

Hint: Traditionally, the sesame burgers are served with sweet chilli sauce. For a change, why not try either hummus, fresh tomato relish or natural yoghurt flavoured with a little mint jelly?

Serves 4 **Calories** 547 **Fat** 30g **Preparation** 10 mins **Cooking** 10 mins

Hint: For a nice alternative, try adding just a little mustard to the mayonnaise and a handful of raisins to the mix.

chicken waldorf *salad wrap*

Serves 4 **Calories** 527
Fat 22g **Preparation** 8 mins

INGREDIENTS

300g cooked chicken, shredded

1 Granny Smith apple, cut into slivers, with a little lemon juice added

1 stalk celery, topped, tailed, then cut into slivers

½ cup chopped walnuts

4 teaspoons mayonnaise

freshly ground black pepper and sea salt to taste

80g iceberg lettuce, shredded

4 Lebanese pita bread wraps

METHOD

1 Combine all of the ingredients other than the lettuce and wraps, and toss gently to combine and coat all ingredients evenly.

2 Divide the mixture between the 4 wraps and top with the lettuce. Roll each wrap to enclose the filling.

poultry
perfection

Hint: A barbecue chicken from your supermarket is great to for use in this recipe – simply ensure you discard any fat or skin!

Hint: Smoked chicken can be used in this recipe. The dressing is simple to prepare and works well with honey and olive oil on salads too.

chicken, asparagus and fetta wrap

INGREDIENTS

1 bunch asparagus
200g cooked chicken, diced
3 truss tomatoes, finely diced
200g fetta cheese, crumbled
salt and pepper to taste
2 cups rocket
4 wholemeal Lebanese flatbread wraps

Serves 4 Calories 493
Fat 18g Preparation 4 mins
Cooking 2 mins

METHOD

1 Trim the woody ends on the asparagus spears, wash spears and place them in a small covered container. Microwave on high for 2 minutes and then cut into bite-sized pieces.

2 Combine all of the ingredients except the wraps in a large bowl, toss gently and divide the salad between the 4 wraps. Roll each wrap to enclose the filling.

turkey and mango wrap

INGREDIENTS

200g smoked turkey, sliced
1 cos lettuce, roughly torn
1 mango, peeled and sliced
1 avocado, sliced
2 teaspoons lemon juice
1 teaspoon wholegrain mustard
salt and pepper to taste
4 mountain bread wraps

METHOD

1 Cut the turkey slices into bite-sized pieces and combine with the cos lettuce, mango and avocado in a large bowl.

2 Place the lemon juice, wholegrain mustard and salt and pepper to taste in a small bowl, and stir to combine. Add the dressing to the turkey mixture and toss gently.

3 Divide the mixture between the wraps and roll each wrap to enclose the filling.

Serves 4 Calories 325 Fat 16g Preparation 4 mins

turkey and mango wrap

asian chicken wrap

Hint: Green prawns, pork fillet or chicken thigh fillets can be used in this recipe to replace the chicken breast fillets.

Serves 4 **Calories** 302
Fat 12g **Preparation** 8 mins
Cooking 10 mins

INGREDIENTS

1 tablespoon peanut oil
500g chicken breast fillets, sliced
1 tablespoon kecap manis
1 tablespoon sweet chilli sauce
140g red cabbage, finely shredded
4 shallots, finely chopped
1 carrot, peeled and grated
1 bunch coriander, finely chopped
1 cup bean sprouts
4 mountain bread wraps

METHOD

1 Heat the peanut oil in a frying pan over a high heat, and stir-fry the chicken for 5 minutes. Add the kecap manis and sweet chilli sauce and stir to coat the chicken.

2 Add the red cabbage, shallots, carrot, coriander and bean sprouts. Stir-fry for 3–5 minutes. Cool slightly and divide the mixture between the wraps. Roll each wrap to enclose the filling. Serve immediately.

honey soy chicken wrap

INGREDIENTS

2 teaspoons peanut oil

500g chicken thigh fillets, cut into strips

1 tablespoon soy sauce

2cm piece fresh ginger, grated

1 clove garlic, crushed

½ teaspoon sesame oil

2 teaspoons honey

140g sugar loaf cabbage, shredded

2 shallots, finely chopped

½ green capsicum, finely chopped

1 carrot, peeled and grated

4 wraps mountain bread

METHOD

1 Heat the peanut oil in a frying pan over a medium heat and fry the chicken until cooked, about 6–8 minutes. Add the soy sauce, ginger, garlic, sesame oil and honey. Stir gently and cook for 2 minutes.

2 Combine the cabbage, shallots, capsicum and carrot in a large bowl, and toss gently.

3 Toss together the chicken mixture and salad and divide between the 4 pieces of mountain bread. Roll the wrap to enclose the filling.

Hint: This filling can also be used in an omelette. It also works well with green prawns instead of chicken.

Serves 4 **Calories** 292
Fat 12g **Preparation** 8 mins
Cooking 10 mins

Hint: Add the pan juices to the salad ingredients to create the dressing. A few chilli flakes added when cooking the chicken will impart a gentle spicy flavour.

Serves 4 Calories 349

Fat 15g Preparation 10 mins

Cooking 5 mins

lemon chicken wrap

INGREDIENTS

2 teaspoons butter
2 teaspoons olive oil
2 chicken breasts, sliced into strips
1 clove garlic, crushed
salt and pepper to taste
juice of 1 lemon
1 cup flat-leaf parsley, finely chopped
4 tortillas
1 cup basil leaves, torn
1 red onion, finely chopped
4 mushrooms, finely chopped

METHOD

1 Heat the butter and oil in a frying pan over a medium heat, and gently fry the chicken, garlic and salt and pepper to taste for 3 minutes. Add the lemon juice and half of the parsley, then cook for a further 2 minutes.

2 Place pieces of chicken onto each tortilla and divide the tossed basil, onion, remaining parsley and mushrooms between each. Roll up each wrap to enclose the filling.

roast chicken and asparagus wrap

INGREDIENTS

1 bunch fresh asparagus

450g cooked chicken

80g iceberg lettuce, shredded

1 bunch chives, finely chopped

2 truss tomatoes, finely diced

salt and pepper to taste

1 tablespoon dijonnaise

4 lavash wraps

4 slices Swiss cheese, cut into strips

METHOD

1 Wash and trim the asparagus of its woody ends. Place in a microwave dish, cover and cook on high for 2 minutes.

2 In a large bowl, combine the chicken, lettuce, chives and tomatoes, plus salt and pepper to taste. Add the Dijonnaise and toss gently.

3 Divide the mixture between the lavash wraps. Top with asparagus spears, 2–3 each, and the Swiss cheese. Roll the wrap to enclose the filling.

Hint: Mayonnaise can be used to replace the dijonnaise. Smoked turkey breast also works well with this recipe.

Serves 4 **Calories** 519

Fat 20g **Preparation** 6 mins

Cooking 2 mins

sweet and mild chicken wrap

Hint: The curry mayonnaise can also be used with canned salmon, prawns, smoked salmon or smoked trout. Make the mayonnaise the day before it's required and refrigerate it – this will further develop the flavour.

INGREDIENTS

1 teaspoon curry powder
½ cup mayonnaise
450g cooked chicken, sliced
80g iceberg lettuce, shredded
1 medium carrot, grated
1 tablespoon sultanas
1 bunch chives, finely chopped
salt and pepper to taste
4 wholemeal Lebanese flatbread wraps

METHOD

1 Stir the curry powder through the mayonnaise and let stand for 10 minutes.

2 In a large bowl, combine the chicken, lettuce, carrot and sultanas. Add the curry mayonnaise, chives and salt and pepper to taste, and toss gently.

3 Divide the mixture between the wraps and roll up each wrap to enclose the filling.

Serves 4 **Calories** 651
Fat 33g **Preparation** 10 mins

tangy chicken wrap

INGREDIENTS

450g cooked chicken, diced
½ cup mayonnaise
2 teaspoons thickened cream
1 teaspoon tamari
2 teaspoons mango chutney
2 stalks celery, finely sliced
2 medium carrots, grated
1 cup parsley, finely chopped
50g shallots, finely chopped
4 lavash bread wraps

METHOD

1 Combine all of the ingredients except the wraps in a large bowl and toss gently.

2 Divide the mixture between the wraps and roll up to enclose the filling.

Hint: Spice up this mixture by adding a small amount of sweet chilli sauce. The mixture may also be served very simply in iceberg lettuce cups.

Serves 4 Calories 619
Fat 33g Preparation 8 mins

269

poultry perfection

Hint: Pesto can be made with a variety of ingredients: cashews, macadamias, walnuts, semi-sun-dried tomatoes and grilled capsicum, to name a few!

Serves 4 Calories 598
Fat 33g Preparation 5 mins

turkey and pesto wrap

INGREDIENTS
½ cup mint leaves
½ cup basil leaves
½ cup flat-leaf parsley
2 cloves garlic
40g Parmesan cheese, grated
⅓ cup almond slivers
⅓ cup extra virgin olive oil
salt and pepper to taste
2 cups mixed salad leaves
1 large tomato, finely chopped
1 onion, finely chopped
200g cooked turkey breast, sliced
4 wholemeal wraps

METHOD

1 Place the mint leaves, basil leaves, flat-leaf parsley, garlic, Parmesan cheese, almond slivers, extra virgin olive oil and salt and pepper to taste in a food processor and blend to a smooth paste.

2 Combine the mixed baby salad leaves, tomato and onion in a bowl and toss gently.

3 Divide the turkey between the wraps and spoon on some of the pesto. Top with the salad and roll each wrap to enclose the filling.

seafood
selection

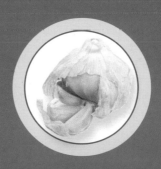

seafood selection

Hint: As an alternative to the prawns, try using poached chicken breast cut into cubes in this recipe.

Hint: Should you prefer a crunchy texture for the fish, simply coat with flour, egg and breadcrumbs after seasoning the fish and then fry as per the recipe.

creamy prawn wrap

INGREDIENTS

1 teaspoon Dijon mustard
1 teaspoon worcestershire sauce
1 clove garlic, crushed
¾ cup mayonnaise
½ bunch chives, finely chopped
2 cups small cooked prawns
40g baby cos lettuce, chopped
2 rashers bacon, grilled and finely chopped
4 lavash wraps

Serves 4 Calories 494
Fat 35g Preparation 5 mins

METHOD

1 Combine the Dijon mustard, worcestershire sauce, garlic, mayonnaise and chives, and process in a food processor until smooth.

2 In a large bowl, combine the mayonnaise mixture, prawns, baby cos lettuce and bacon, and toss gently. Divide the mixture between the wraps and roll each wrap to enclose the filling.

thai fish wrap

INGREDIENTS

400g firm white fish fillets, cut into strips
2 teaspoons Thai seasoning
2 teaspoons peanut oil
juice of 1 lemon or lime
1 bunch coriander, finely chopped
2cm piece fresh ginger, grated
1 red capsicum, finely chopped
½ cup mint, chopped
½ cup Thai basil, chopped
1 red onion, finely sliced
4 mountain bread wraps

METHOD

1 Combine the coriander, capsicum, mint, Thai basil and red onion in a bowl and toss to mix well.

2 Sprinkle the fish strips with the Thai seasoning and fry in the peanut oil on medium heat for 3–4 minutes each side.

3 Sprinkle with the lime or lemon juice and ginger.

4 Divide the salad between the mountain bread wraps and top with a few pieces of fish and some of the pan juices. Roll up the mountain bread to enclose the filling.

Serves 4 Calories 208 Fat 5g
Preparation 6 mins Cooking 6 mins

thai fish wrap

Hint: This garlic prawn mixture is also delicious stirred through cooked penne or cooked rice.

Serves 4 **Calories** 363
Fat 13g **Preparation** 10 mins
Cooking 3 mins

garlic prawn and lime wrap

INGREDIENTS

2 teaspoons butter
2 tablespoons olive oil
16 green prawns, peeled and deveined
4 cloves garlic, crushed
½ teaspoon chilli flakes
juice of 1 lime
salt and pepper to taste
1 bunch coriander, roughly chopped
2 cups rocket
1 large tomato, finely chopped
1 cup bean sprouts
1 red onion, finely chopped
4 lavash wraps

METHOD

1 In a frying pan over a medium heat, heat the butter and the oil, until sizzling.

2 Add the prawns, garlic and chilli flakes. Cook, stirring constantly, until the prawns change colour, 3–5 minutes.

3 Add the lime juice and salt and pepper to taste.

4 Combine all of the salad ingredients in a large bowl and toss well. Add the prawns and the pan juices to the salad and toss to combine.

5 Divide the mixture between the 4 lavash wraps. Roll to enclose the filling and serve immediately.

light and lovely salmon wrap

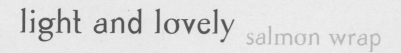

INGREDIENTS

200g smoked salmon, chopped

2 cups rocket

1 avocado, finely diced

1 bunch chives, finely chopped

1 punnet grape tomatoes, quartered

½ cup basil, chopped

1 tablespoon lime juice

1 tablespoon extra virgin olive oil

Lebanese cucumber, finely chopped

salt and pepper to taste

4 wholemeal Lebanese flatbread wraps

METHOD

1 Combine all of the ingredients, except the wraps, in a large bowl and toss gently.

2 Divide the mixture between the wraps and roll up to enclose the filling.

Hint: Cooked small prawns, smoked chicken or smoked turkey can be used in this healthy recipe.

Serves 4 **Calories** 440

Fat 18g **Preparation** 10 mins

crispy fish tortilla

crispy fish tortilla

INGREDIENTS

400g firm white fish fillets, cut into strips
1 teaspoon lemon pepper seasoning
1 tablespoon plain flour
1 egg, lightly beaten and mixed with ⅓ cup milk
1½ cups fine dry breadcrumbs
½ cup olive oil
1 iceberg lettuce, shredded
1 punnet grape tomatoes, halved
4 tortillas
1 avocado, mashed with the juice of ½ lemon
mayonnaise to taste
100g shallots, finely chopped
salt and pepper to taste
lemon wedges, to serve

METHOD

1 Sprinkle the fish strips with lemon pepper seasoning, dust with flour, dip in egg mixture and coat well with breadcrumbs.

2 Fry fish in olive oil on medium heat until golden, about 3 minutes each side.

3 Combine the lettuce and tomatoes and toss well. Spread each tortilla with avocado mixture.

4 Divide the salad between the tortillas.

5 Divide the fish strips between the tortillas and top with mayonnaise, shallots and salt and pepper to taste. Roll the tortillas to enclose the filling. Serve with lemon wedges.

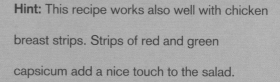

beyond the fish finger

I am blessed with two beautiful boys – Jeff and Grant. One loves fishing and one loves cooking. Jeff has the boat and all the fishing gear and manages to catch some great eating fish. Grant loves to cook and came up with this tasty recipe to make good use of the fresh fish. The lovely, crisp strips of fish are a long way from the fish fingers they loved as children! My passion for food has flowed on to the boys in much the same way as it did to me from my grandmother. I wasn't taught to cook, but learnt by observing. My interest was further fuelled by always enjoying the end result! Every meal was an event when I was growing up, and I've endeavoured to make sure it's the same for my family.

Hint: This recipe works also well with chicken breast strips. Strips of red and green capsicum add a nice touch to the salad.

277

Serves 4 Calories 810 Fat 53g Preparation 12 mins Cooking 6 mins

prawn cocktail wrap

Hint: For a spicy flavour try adding a little Tabasco or mustard.

Serves 4 **Calories** 183
Fat 4g **Preparation** 5 mins

INGREDIENTS

2 cups small cooked prawns
1 tablespoon sour cream
2 teaspoons mayonnaise
1 teaspoon tomato sauce
squeeze lemon juice
freshly ground black pepper
and sea salt to taste
½ small bunch chives, finely chopped
½ cup parsley, finely chopped
1 cup rocket
80g iceberg lettuce, shredded
4 mountain bread wraps

METHOD

1 Combine all of the ingredients other than the rocket, lettuce and the wraps, and toss gently.

2 Divide the mixture between the 4 wraps and top with the lettuce and rocket. Roll each wrap to enclose the filling.

smoked salmon gourmet wrap

INGREDIENTS

2 tablespoons cream cheese

2 teaspoons baby capers

2 gherkins

juice of 1 lemon

80g Mesclun leaves

1 red capsicum, finely chopped

1 red onion, finely chopped

½ cup semi-sun-dried tomatoes, very finely chopped

2 teaspoons olive oil

4 mountain bread wraps

100g smoked salmon

METHOD

1 Combine the cream cheese, baby capers, gherkins and half of the lemon juice in a small food processor and blend until smooth.

2 In a large bowl, mix together the Mesclun leaves, capsicum, onion and semi-sun-dried tomatoes. Add the lemon juice and olive oil. Toss to coat the salad.

3 Spread the cream cheese mixture onto the 4 pieces of mountain bread. Divide the salad between mountain bread and top with 2–3 slices of smoked salmon. Roll up to enclose the filling. Cut in half to serve.

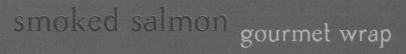

Hint: Cooked prawns can also be used in this recipe.

Serves 4 **Calories** 204
Fat 7g **Preparation** 5 mins

tangy tuna wrap

tangy tuna wrap

INGREDIENTS

300g canned tuna in extra
virgin olive oil

3 cups rocket

2 teaspoons lemon juice

1 Lebanese cucumber,
finely chopped

1 red onion, finely sliced

1/2 cup semi-sun-dried tomatoes,
finely chopped

freshly ground black pepper
and sea salt to taste

4 wholemeal Lebanese
flatbread wraps

mayonnaise to taste

2 teaspoons baby capers

METHOD

1 Flake the tuna but do not drain.

2 In a large bowl, combine the tuna with the rocket, lemon juice, cucumber, onion and semi-sun-dried tomatoes then add salt and pepper to taste.

3 Divide the tuna and salad mixture between the wraps. Top with a little mayonnaise and some baby capers. Roll the wraps to enclose the filling.

Hint: Use any of the flavoured tuna varieties now readily available in supermarkets for an extra boost of flavour in this recipe.

Serves 4 **Calories** 503 **Fat** 23g **Preparation** 4 mins

tuna and watercress wrap

Hint: The full-bodied flavour obtained from cooking fresh tuna is certainly worth the effort, Once you've tried fresh tuna in this wrap the chances are you won't settle for anything less!

INGREDIENTS

200g fresh tuna
2 teaspoons extra virgin olive oil
1½ cups watercress
10 cherry tomatoes, halved
1 cup bean sprouts
50g shallots, finely chopped
½ cup walnut pieces
¼ cup walnut oil
1 tablespoon apple cider vinegar
1 teaspoon tamari
freshly ground black pepper
4 lavash wraps

METHOD

1 In a non-stick frying pan on a medium heat, sauté the tuna in olive oil for 2 minutes each side. Allow it to rest for 5 minutes.

2 Combine the watercress, tomatoes, bean sprouts, shallots, walnut pieces, walnut oil, apple cider vinegar, tamari and black pepper to taste. Toss gently.

3 Dice the tuna and divide between the wraps. Top with the salad and roll each wrap to enclose the filling.

Serves 4 **Calories** 613
Fat 41g **Preparation** 12 mins
Cooking 4 mins

deli delight

deli delight

Hint: Snowpea sprouts, capsicum, tomato, celery, grated carrot and rocket can also be used in this tasty wrap to increase its nutritional value.

This recipe also lends itself to a variety of cheeses such as Swiss, Edam or soft vintage Cheddar.

Hint: Hummus, salsa or pesto can be used to replace the avocado.

turkey, cranberry *and avocado wrap*

INGREDIENTS

80g Mesclun leaves

1 Lebanese cucumber, finely chopped

1 red onion, finely chopped

salt and black pepper to taste

1 avocado, mashed with lemon juice

4 lavash wraps

150g cooked turkey breast, sliced

2 tablespoons cranberry sauce

4 slices Jarlsberg cheese

dijonnaise to taste

Serves 4 Calories 515

Fat 27g Preparation 4 mins

METHOD

1 Combine the Mesclun leaves, cucumber, onion and s and pepper to taste.

2 Spread the avocado mixture onto the 4 wraps. Top w turkey, cranberry sauce, cheese and salad. Drizzle a littl dijonnaisse onto each one. Roll up the wraps to enclose the filling.

brie, ham *and avocado wrap*

INGREDIENTS

4 wholemeal Lebanese flatbreads

1 avocado, mashed with lemon juice

200g double smoked leg ham

250g Brie cheese, sliced

3 cups watercress

½ red capsicum, finely sliced

1 carrot, peeled and grated

1 small cucumber, chopped

1 teaspoon olive oil

2 teaspoons lemon juice

salt and pepper to taste

METHOD

1 Spread each of the wraps with the mashed avocado then top with ham and the Brie cheese slices.

2 Combine the watercress, capsicum, carrot, cucumbe olive oil, lemon juice and salt and pepper to taste. Toss gently and divide between the 4 wraps. Roll each wrap t enclose the filling.

Serves 4 Calories 644 Fat 37g Preparation 4 min

brie, ham and avocado wrap

deli delight

Hint: This tasty filling can be used as a pizza topping: just omit the rocket. Any deli meats and small quantities of vegetables can be used.

Serves 4 **Calories** 476
Fat 20g **Preparation** 20 mins

deli and *vegie sensation*

INGREDIENTS

100g salami, finely diced
100g smoked ham, finely diced
1 red onion, thinly sliced
1 green capsicum, finely diced
2 cloves garlic, crushed
6 button mushrooms, sliced
2 tomatoes, finely diced
40g Parmesan cheese, grated
1 tablespoon olive oil
½ teaspoon chilli flakes
salt and pepper to taste
2 cups rocket
4 wholemeal wraps

METHOD

1 Combine all of the ingredients except the wraps. Refrigerate for 10 minutes or more to develop the flavours.

2 Divide the mixture between the wraps and roll each wrap to enclose the filling.

ham, cheese and olive wrap

INGREDIENTS

1 cup green olives stuffed
with anchovies

2 tablespoons extra virgin olive oil

1 tablespoon mint leaves, chopped

1 tablespoon baby capers

freshly ground black pepper

1 anchovy

3 cups mixed salad leaves

1 medium carrot, grated

1 Lebanese cucumber, finely sliced

½ cup semi-sun-dried tomatoes,
finely chopped

300g lean leg ham, sliced

6 slices Swiss cheese

4 lavash or mountain bread wraps

METHOD

1 Combine the olives, olive oil, mint leaves, capers, black pepper and anchovy in a small food processor, and blend until finely chopped.

2 Toss together the mixed leaves, carrot, cucumber and semi sun-dried tomatoes.

3 Divide the ham, Swiss cheese and olive mixture between the 4 wraps, then top with the salad. Roll each wrap to enclose the filling.

Hint: Mixed leaves are a combination of Mesclun, spinach and rocket. Black olives can also be used in this recipe.

Serves 4 **Calories** 553
Fat 27g **Preparation** 8 mins

deli delight

Hint: Lean bacon can be used instead of the pancetta, semi-sun-dried tomatoes can replace the truss tomatoes and Mozzarella cheese may be used as an alternative to the baby bocconcini. Mixed leaves can be substituted for the rocket.

italian deli wrap

INGREDIENTS

8 slices pancetta, grilled
1 cup basil leaves, roughly torn
80g rocket, roughly chopped
2 teaspoons lemon juice
1 tablespoon extra virgin olive oil
freshly ground black pepper and sea salt
4 truss tomatoes, sliced
4 lavash wraps
16 baby bocconcini cheeses

METHOD

1 Combine the basil leaves, rocket, lemon juice, olive oil and salt and pepper to taste in a bowl, and toss gently.

2 Lay slices of tomato onto each wrap and top with a portion of the salad.

3 Crumble the grilled pancetta onto each wrap, followed by a 4 baby bocconcini cheeses. Roll each wrap to enclose the filling.

Serves 4 **Calories** 537
Fat 27g **Preparation** 6 mins

new york roast wrap

INGREDIENTS

3 cups watercress

2 teaspoons balsamic vinegar

1 tablespoon olive oil

2 teaspoons walnut oil

½ cup walnut pieces

1 bunch garlic chives, finely chopped

salt and pepper to taste

200g rare roast beef, sliced

4 lavash wraps

1 tablespoon horseradish cream

METHOD

1 In a bowl, combine the watercress, balsamic vinegar, olive oil, walnut oil, walnut pieces, chives and salt and pepper to taste and toss gently.

2 Place 50g of rare roast beef on each wrap. Spread each with 1 teaspoon of horseradish cream. Divide the salad between the 4 wraps and roll the wraps to enclose the filling.

Hint: For a more substantial meal, use home-cooked, thick-cut roast beef. Roast lamb and hummus can also be used.

Serves 4 **Calories** 442
Fat 22g **Preparation** 6 mins

deli delight

Hint: Most varieties of wrap can be successfully cooked in a sandwich press to create a hot, crispy light meal.

Serves 4 Calories 415
Fat 29g Preparation 5 mins
Cooking 10 mins

pepperoni and asparagus wrap

INGREDIENTS

1 bunch asparagus
200g pepperoni, thinly sliced
4 tortillas
8 slices mozzarella cheese
1 red onion, sliced
1 red capsicum, thinly sliced
80g spinach
salt and pepper to taste

METHOD

1 Preheat a sandwich press.

2 Trim the woody ends off the asparagus and rinse the trimmed spears in cold water. Cook the asparagus in a small covered container for 2 minutes on high in a microwave oven.

3 Divide the pepperoni between the tortillas, then top with 2 slices of mozzarella cheese and a few asparagus spears.

4 Combine the onion, capsicum, spinach, salt and pepper to taste. Divide between the tortillas and roll each wrap to enclose the filling. Place the filled tortillas in the hot sandwich press and cook for 6–8 minutes.

roast pork
with special sauce wrap

INGREDIENTS

2 cups mixed salad leaves
2 truss tomatoes, finely chopped
1 bunch chives, finely chopped
2 teaspoons lemon juice
2 teaspoons olive oil
1 tablespoon apple sauce
2 teaspoons cranberry sauce
1 teaspoon balsamic vinegar
2 teaspoons brown sugar
salt and pepper to taste
200g roast pork, sliced
4 mountain bread wraps

METHOD

1 Combine the salad ingredients, lemon juice and olive oil in a bowl, then toss gently.

2 Combine the apple sauce, cranberry sauce, balsamic vinegar, brown sugar and salt and pepper to taste in a small saucepan. Simmer on low heat for 5 minutes, and allow to cool before using.

3 Divide the roast pork between the wraps. Top with the special sauce and salad and roll each wrap to enclose the filling.

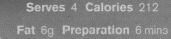

Hint: This special sauce also works well with leg ham, turkey and chicken and leftover pork roast.

Serves 4 **Calories** 212
Fat 6g **Preparation** 6 mins

deli delight

Hint: Combine 2 teaspoons of red wine vinegar, 2 teaspoons honey and 1 tablespoon of olive oil to make a dressing. Add extra grated apple and chopped cos lettuce to make a wonderful salad.

deli chicken, mushroom and almond wrap

INGREDIENTS

120g smoked chicken breast, diced

½ small Granny Smith apple, grated with 1 tablespoon lemon juice

1 stalk celery, finely sliced

½ cup parsley, finely chopped

1 tablespoon coleslaw dressing

2 cups blanched almonds, roasted and chopped

3 mushroooms, sliced and pan-fried

4 tortillas

METHOD

1 Combine the chicken, apple, celery, parsley, mushrooms and dressing.

2 Divide the mixture between the 4 tortillas and top with the almonds and mushrooms. Roll up to enclose the filling.

Serves 4 **Calories** 603
Fat 47g **Preparation** 5 mins

292

hearty
meats

Hint: Leftover cooked meat or chicken can be used in this recipe – it's great for barbecue leftovers! Include sour cream, mashed avocado and chilli sauce for extra flavour and zing!

Hint: Spoon a little tomato salsa onto each patty for extra flavour.

hot toasted sausage wrap

INGREDIENTS

8 beef or pork sausages
4 tortillas
1 onion, finely chopped
½ cup tomato salsa
60g Cheddar cheese, grated
2 cups spinach
salt and pepper to taste

Serves 4 Calories 578
Fat 45g Preparation 5 mins
Cooking 20 mins

METHOD

1 Barbecue or pan-fry the sausages.

2 Place 2 sausages on to each tortilla. Top with a little chopped onion, salsa and grated cheese, then place some of the spinach onto each tortilla, and season to taste. Roll the tortillas to enclose the filling.

3 Place the tortillas onto a preheated sandwich press; and cook for 6–8 minutes.

aussie burger wrap

INGREDIENTS

200g lean beef mince
1 onion, finely chopped
1 teaspoon dried oregano leaves
salt and pepper to taste
80g iceberg lettuce, shredded
1 Lebanese cucumber, sliced
2 tomatoes, sliced
4 mountain bread wraps
4 slices Cheddar cheese, halved
barbecue sauce or tomato sauce

METHOD

1 Form the mince into 4 beef patties. In a frying pan on high heat, dry-fry the patties, pressing them down to make them thin. Press some onion into each one. Sprinkle over the oregano leaves and add salt and pepper to taste. Turn the patties after 3 minutes and cook for a further 3 minutes.

2 Combine the lettuce, cucumber and tomatoes in a bowl. Divide the salad between the 4 wraps, top with a beef patty, sauce and a cheese slice. Roll each wrap to enclose the filling.

Serves 4 Calories 251 Fat 11g Preparation 15 mins Cooking 6 mins

aussie burger wrap

295

Hint: A small amount of horseradish cream can also be added to the mayonnaise.

Serves 4 **Calories** 462
Fat 20g **Preparation** 5 mins
Cooking 15 mins

chorizo, potato and dill wrap

INGREDIENTS

2 medium sebago potatoes, peeled

3 chorizos, sliced diagonally

2 teaspoons fresh dill leaves, finely chopped

⅓ cup mayonnaise

½ red onion, finely chopped

salt and pepper to taste

4 wholemeal Lebanese flatbread wraps

2 cups rocket

METHOD

1 Steam the potatoes until cooked but still firm, and allow to cool.

2 In a frying pan, fry the sausage pieces until browned on both sides.

3 Combine the potatoes, dill leaves, mayonnaise, onion and salt and pepper to taste, and toss gently.

4 Divide the mixture between the 4 wraps and top with the sausage pieces and rocket. Roll up each wrap to enclose the filling.

corned beef and potato wrap

INGREDIENTS

1 large onion, chopped

2 medium potatoes, diced

2 teaspoons olive oil

200g cooked corned beef, cut into bite-sized pieces

½ cup parsley, finely chopped

salt and pepper to taste

2 cups mixed lettuce

4 Lebanese flatbread wraps

2 tablespoons fruit chutney

METHOD

1 In a frying pan, cook the onion and potato in olive oil until almost cooked. Add the corned beef and parsley, then heat gently for 5 minutes. Add salt and pepper to taste.

2 Divide the lettuce between the wraps. Top with the corned beef mixture and a spoonful of chutney. Roll each wrap to enclose the filling.

Hint: Leftover roast lamb can be used in place of the corned beef. Vary the recipes with any of the relishes and pickles you like.

Serves 4 **Calories** 402
Fat 8g **Preparation** 6 mins
Cooking 8 mins

297

pastrami delight

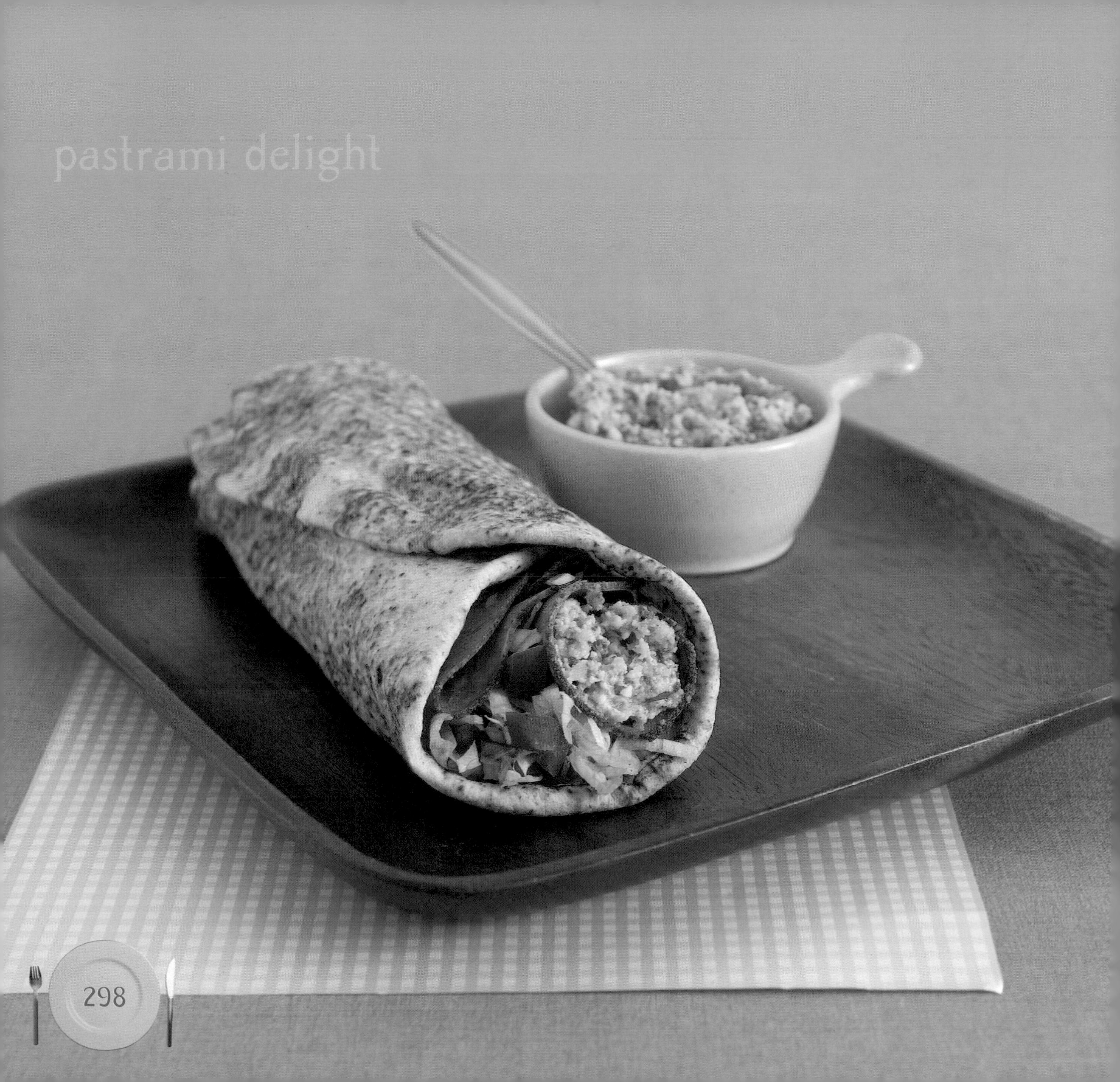

pastrami delight

INGREDIENTS

½ cup macadamia nuts

1 clove garlic

2 teaspoons baby capers

2 gherkins

½ cup parsley, finely chopped

⅓ cup extra virgin olive oil

salt and pepper to taste

120g iceberg lettuce, finely shredded

1 truss tomato, finely chopped

small red onion, finely chopped

200g pastrami

4 Lebanese flatbread wraps

Serves 4 **Calories** 620

Fat 37g **Preparation** 6 mins

METHOD

1 Place macadamias, garlic, capers, gherkins, parsley and olive oil in a small food processor, add salt and pepper to taste and process to a purée.

2 Combine the iceberg lettuce, tomato and red onion in a bowl.

3 Place 50g pastrami onto each wrap and top with the nut purée and salad. Roll each wrap to enclose the filling.

at the deli

Finding a quality continental-style delicatessen is like finding gold. Your deli owner can become your best friend and share their vast knowledge to help you make a selection.

Like all smoked meats, pastrami has become more popular over the last decade. What I love about pastrami it is rich flavour and its ability to turn a simple wrap into a gourmet treat. We've come a long way since the days of rather ordinary smoked meats! Whilst beef continues to be the most popular pastrami meat, turkey pastrami is now offered, along with venison and duck. There's even a vegetarian pastrami, made of vegetables and wheat flour.

Pastrami is typically used in sandwiches but it's also delicious warm with a side dish such as a mixed slaw or potato salad.

nt: Corned beef, salami or any spicy sausage will work well in this recipe.

r a change, use walnuts, almonds or cashews instead of the macadamias.

marvellous meat

Hint: Lamb or pork fillets work well as an alternative to the rump steak.

Serves 4 Calories 418
Fat 11.3g Preparation 6 mins
Cooking 10 mins

warm steak wrap

INGREDIENTS

400g lean rump steak
2 teaspoons butter
2 teaspoons olive oil
1 clove garlic, crushed
1 tablespoon balsamic vinegar
6 semi-sun-dried tomatoes
1½ teaspoons Dijon mustard
½ cup fresh basil leaves, chopped
salt and pepper to taste
80g cos lettuce
2 shallots
4 Lebanese flatbread wraps

METHOD

1 Pan-fry the steak in the butter, olive oil and garlic for 4 minutes each side. Allow the steak to rest for 5 minutes.

2 Process the balsamic vinegar, the semi-sun-dried tomatoes, mustard, basil leaves and salt and pepper to taste in a food processor until finely chopped.

3 Combine the cos lettuce and shallots in a bowl. Thinly slice the steak, add the pan juices to the lettuce and shallots, and toss gently.

4 Divide the steak between the wraps and top with some of the tomato mix. Finally, add the lettuce mix to the wraps and roll each wrap to enclose the filling.

moroccan lamb wrap

INGREDIENTS

1 tablespoon olive oil

1 tablespoon butter

3 cloves garlic, crushed

6 lamb chump chops

1 tablespoon Moroccan-style seasoning

80g mixed salad leaves

juice of 1 lemon or lime

4 pita wraps

METHOD

1 Heat a frying pan and add olive oil, butter, garlic, lamb and seasoning.

2 Stir-fry for a few minutes until cooked. Add lamb, plus the pan juices, to the salad mix. Toss well to combine and squeeze over lemon or lime juice.

3 Place a quarter of the filling in the centre of each pita and wrap.

Hint: Open your pita bread wraps at the last minute and fill them just before eating, to keep them fresh and soft.

Serves 4 Calories 457

Fat 19g Preparation 5 mins

Cooking 5 mins

Hint: You can substitute chicken or pork for the beef. You can also use Lebanese bread or tortillas for the wraps.

Serves 4   Calories 561
Fat 29g   Preparation 5 mins
Cooking 10 mins

beef wraps

INGREDIENTS

2 tablespoons plain flour
1 teaspoon smoked paprika
400g rump beef, thinly sliced
⅓ cup vegetable oil
4 lavash wraps
1 carrot, grated
1 Lebanese cucumber, sliced
40g Cheddar cheese, grated
40g iceberg lettuce, shredded
barbecue sauce to taste

METHOD

1 Combine the flour and paprika in a bowl. Coat the steak lightly in the flour.

2 Heat half the oil in a large frying pan over medium – high heat. Cook the beef in 2 batches for 3–4 minutes or until cooked.

3 Top the lavash bread with carrot, cucumber, cheese, lettuce, steak and a drizzle of barbecue sauce. Roll up and cut in half.

Brenda Kitchen's

COMFORT FOOD

On the table

in 20 minutes

R&R PUBLICATIONS MARKETING PTY LTD

contents

introduction   306

marvellous meats   309

tasty chicken   323

sensational seafood   335

easy vegetables   343

extraordinary eggs   343

delicious desserts   353

tantalising sauces   362

Introduction
Comfort food

The inspiration for my book comes from almost 20 years of creating recipes for 'Simply Cooking' and from my wonderful nan!

'Simply Cooking' is the name of my fresh food company, which for more than 20 years has provided a service to major shopping centres throughout New South Wales. My loyal sponsors have supported my idea that simple, home-cooked food has widespread appeal.

After much positive feedback from my fresh food promotions and hundreds of great recipes, the time was perfect for "On the Table in 20 Minutes". These comfort food recipes, using fresh produce and simple methods, are now part of a series of six books.

For as long as I can remember, food has meant more to me than merely a way to satisfy hunger. Food is my life passion. In 'Comfort Food', you will discover recipes that are fast and fabulous, plus slow, tasty winter warmers such as Brenda's Irish stew. With comfort in mind, this book is a mixture of fast and slow offerings.

I hope you enjoy cooking my recipes, and may the aromas of real comfort food fill your kitchen and delight you as they do me.

Cooking with feeling ~ Brenda

A warm and *wonderful world*

My nan played a part inspiring me to write this book. She created for me a warm and wonderful world in which food played a huge role.

My brother Brian and I lived with Nan and Pa from when we were very young. We were raised in Clovelly, a seaside suburb of Sydney. The beach was a short stroll down the steep hill of Melrose Parade, and I have fond memories of long summer days spent at the beach with my friends and returning home to good old-fashioned meals. I remember that Nan always cooked the best roast dinners for Sunday lunch. There's nothing like the smell and taste of a roast dinner after spending a morning at the beach – days of true comfort!

The Sunday roast consisted mainly of lamb with crispy baked potatoes, pumpkin, fresh beans and, of course, lots of gravy. It was always a home-made gravy, not the bought stuff some like to call gravy. Gravy really completes a roast dinner, and it's so easy to make with some simple ingredients and a little patience. Combining 20-minute meals with some old-fashioned home cooking is a perfect way to balance your time in the kitchen.

Food has always inspired my imagination

marvellous
meats

Hint: Irish stew is delicious, but you must use the best neck lamb chops. I'm not sure why their flavour is so very different from other lamb chops, but I have found that if you don't use neck chops, you don't get the same flavour. If you want to make your stew extra creamy, add a little milk to the dish.

Hint: Usually chilli con carne has red kidney beans but I've chosen to use the three bean mix. It gives the dish a lovely flavour and different look and texture. It really tastes fantastic!

310

brenda's *irish stew*

INGREDIENTS

8 best neck lamb chops
3 large old potatoes, peeled and sliced thickly
2 large carrots, sliced
½ cup fresh parsley, chopped
salt and pepper to taste
2 tablespoons plain flour
a little milk, optional

Serves 4 **Calories** 425
Fat 8.2 **Preparation** 10 mins
Cooking 1 hr 40 mins

METHOD

1 Preheat the oven to 180°C. Layer the chops, potatoes, carrots and parsley in a casserole dish. Season to taste and cover with boiling water. Put the lid on the casserole and cook in the oven for 1½ hours.

2 Thicken by mixing the plain flour with a little sauce from the stew. Stir into the stew and place back into the oven for a further 10 minutes. For a creamy gravy, replace some of the liquid from the stew with a little milk after cooking.

chilli *con carne*

INGREDIENTS

1 onion, finely chopped
1 clove garlic, crushed
1 tablespoon olive oil
500g extra-lean beef mince
500g medium-hot tomato salsa
425g canned three bean mix, drained
1 bay leaf
1 green capsicum, finely chopped
½ cup beef stock
salt and pepper to taste

METHOD

1 Gently fry the onion and garlic in the olive oil until softened. Add the mince and cook until it changes colour.

2 Add the remaining ingredients and simmer for 40 minutes. Serve with corn chips, grated cheese, sour cream and guacamole.

Variation: Create nachos by lining a baking dish with corn chips and topping with chilli con carne and grated cheese. Bake at 180°C for 20 minutes.

Serves 4 **Calories** 511 **Fat** 7.5 **Preparation** 10 mins **Cooking** 45 mins

chilli con carne

pasta bake

pasta bake

INGREDIENTS

1 large onion, chopped
1 clove garlic, crushed
150g lean bacon, chopped
3 large mushrooms, chopped
1 teaspoon ground paprika
1 teaspoon oregano leaves
1 tablespoon olive oil
500g lean beef mince
300g tomato salsa
½ red capsicum, chopped
1 cup basil leaves, chopped
2 bay leaves
500g spaghetti, cooked and drained
500g Cheddar cheese, grated

topping

80g Cheddar cheese, grated
2 eggs, beaten
cup fresh breadcrumbs, toasted

METHOD

1 Preheat the oven to 180°C. Fry the onion, garlic, bacon, mushrooms, paprika and oregano in the olive oil until softened.

2 Add the beef mince and cook over a high heat until it changes colour and breaks into small pieces.

3 Add the salsa, capsicum, basil and bay leaves. Simmer for 30 minutes.

4 Layer the spaghetti with the meat sauce and cheese into a large, shallow baking dish.

5 To make the topping, combine the cheese with the eggs. Pour over the top of spaghetti bake, then sprinkle with the breadcrumbs.

6 Bake for 30 minutes until golden brown. Serve with a crisp green salad.

Hint: Any variety of salsa or flavoured Italian-style tomato sauces can be used to make a good pasta bake. Keep your eye out for new varieties on the supermarket shelf.

Serves 6 **Calories** 611 **Fat** 9.7 **Preparation** 10 mins **Cooking** 1 hr 10 mins

313

Hint: Serve with creamy mashed potato and a green vegetable. This also makes a wonderful winter pie with some pre-made shortcrust pastry.

Hint: If you like spicy pepper steak, then use a generous amount of seasoned pepper or pepper steak seasoning. Make sure to use a tender cut of meat, such as rump steak, T-bone or sirloin.

hearty stew

INGREDIENTS

1kg stewing steak, cubed
2 tablespoons plain flour
2 teaspoons sugar
3 onions, sliced
1 teaspoon crushed garlic
200g lean bacon, finely chopped
1 tablespoon olive oil
1 tablespoon worcestershire sauce
2 tablespoons malt vinegar
300g tomato salsa
sea salt
cracked black peppercorns

Serves 6 **Calories** 328

Fat 4.7g **Preparation** 10 mins

Cooking 2 hrs 10 mins

METHOD

1 Coat the stewing steak in flour and sugar and set aside.

2 In a large heavy-based frying pan, fry the onions, garlic and bacon in the olive oil until softened. Add the stewing steak and cook for a few minutes to seal in the flavour.

3 Add the rest of the ingredients, season to taste and simmer for 2 hours.

creamy pepper steak

INGREDIENTS

1 tablespoon butter
500g rump steak, trimmed
sprinkle of black pepper
¼ red parsley and chives, chopped
3 tablespoons cream
salt and pepper to taste

Serves 2 **Calories** 108.5

Fat 3.4g **Preparation** 5 mins

Cooking 10 mins

METHOD

1 Melt the butter in a frying pan and add the rump steak and lightly sprinkle with pepper. Cook until lightly browned, then turn and lightly sprinkle the other side with the pepper.

2 Before the rump steak is cooked, add the parsley and chives. Then add the cream. If you want a lot of sauce, add all the cream. If only a little sauce is required, add only 1 or 2 tablespoons of cream.

3 Turn the rump steak several times in the sauce, season to taste, then serve.

creamy pepper steak

basic pie filling

basic pie *filling*

INGREDIENTS

500g lean beef mince
1 medium onion, finely chopped
salt and pepper to taste
1 teaspoon mixed herbs
1 cup water
Parisienne essence, to colour
2 tablespoons plain flour, mixed
to a paste with water

METHOD

1 Place the mince, half the onion, salt and pepper, mixed herbs, water and a few drops of Parisienne essence into a saucepan and bring to the boil.

2 Reduce the heat to a simmer, cover the saucepan and cook for 30 minutes.

3 Add the rest of the onion and the flour mixture to the mince a little at a time until thickened. Adjust seasonings if necessary.

Serves 4 **Calories** 288 **Fat** 7.7g **Preparation** 30 mins **Cooking** 35 mins

nt: Parisienne essence is a colouring agent available at your supermarket. Add ore colouring, if needed, to give a rich brown gravy. Use this filling for meat pies th shortcrust pastry. Cook pies in a preheated oven at 220°C until golden, around minutes. Nan always decorated her pies with pastry leaves and glazed the top th milk mixed with an egg yolk.

a meat pie story

During the 50s in the seaside suburb of Coogee, Sydney, stood the famous Coogee Pie Shop. This unpretentious shop sold the most delicious pies with fine crisp pastry and a generous filling of rich gravy and mince.

Nan's pies are the closest to the famous Coogee Pie. Many gourmet pies are available today, but the basic meat pie is still the most sought-after by Aussie pie eaters.

A home-made meat pie can be served with seasonal vegetables for a tasty and nutritious meal. Pre-made shortcrust pastry makes pie-making simple. Individual non-stick pie dishes are available in good kitchen shops and some department stores.

On baking days, Nan would make cakes, biscuits and pies for the coming week's meals. The perfect leaves cut from the pastry to decorate the pies always fascinated me and I still make them for my pies today. They bring back warm memories of baking days during my childhood.

317

Hint: When using lamb chump chops, take all the lean meat off the bone. Discard the bone and visible fat. This is a very simple dish, yet it tastes fantastic and is a healthy and casual meal.

Serves 4 **Calories** 210
Fat 2.3g **Preparation** 10 mins
Cooking 10 mins

moroccan lamb salad wraps

INGREDIENTS

**500g lean lamb, cut from
6–8 lamb chump chops**
sprinkle of Moroccan-style seasoning
1 tablespoon olive oil
mixed salad leaves
a few chopped mint leaves
3 tomatoes, sliced
Lebanese cucumber, thinly sliced
1 medium red onion, sliced
1 red capsicum, thinly sliced
juice of 2 lemons
1 tablespoon olive oil
Lebanese or lavash bread

METHOD

1 Sprinkle the sliced lamb with Moroccan seasoning and fry in the olive oil for a few minutes, but don't overcook.

2 Combine the lamb with all the remaining ingredients except the bread.

3 Put a generous amount of the lamb and salad mixture into the Lebanese or lavash bread and serve immediately

mini meaty balls

INGREDIENTS

750g lean mince
1cm piece ginger, freshly chopped
1 bunch fresh chives, chopped
½ bunch fresh coriander, chopped
1 egg
sprinkle of garlic steak seasoning
dry breadcrumbs, to coat

METHOD

1 Preheat a large frying pan. Mix all the ingredients except the breadcrumbs in a bowl. Using a dessertspoon, form small balls. Coat the meaty balls with the dry breadcrumbs.

2 Dry-fry the meaty balls for 8–10 minutes, turning every couple of minutes.

Hint: This is a lovely recipe if you want to serve mini cocktail meaty balls before dinner. With a few basic ingredients, including the mince, fresh ginger and fresh coriander, you're giving your mini meaty balls lots of flavour. Next time you're having a party, serve some mini meaty balls each on toothpicks.

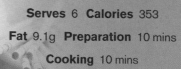

Serves 6 **Calories** 353
Fat 9.1g **Preparation** 10 mins
Cooking 10 mins

supreme bolognese

Serves 4 **Calories** 98
Fat 0.7g **Preparation** 10 mins
Cooking 40 mins

INGREDIENTS

1 tablespoon olive oil
1 large brown onion, finely chopped
2 cloves garlic, crushed
70g lean bacon, chopped
500g extra-lean beef mince
1 teaspoon ground paprika
pinch of sugar
400g canned whole Roma tomatoes
2 tablespoons tomato paste
200g mushrooms, chopped
½ cup fresh basil, chopped
¼ teaspoon chilli flakes
½ cup red wine
½ teaspoon sea salt
½ teaspoon cracked black peppercorns

METHOD

1 Heat an frying pan. Add the olive oil, onion, garlic and bacon and cook until softened. Add the mince and cook until it changes colour, breaking the mince up with a fork as you are cooking.

2 Add all the remaining ingredients and simmer until cooked, for about 30 minutes. Serve with freshly cooked spaghetti.

320

rich and tasty pork chops

INGREDIENTS

2 teaspoons olive oil
4 large pork chops
1 large onion, chopped
2 cloves garlic, crushed
1 stalk chopped celery
½ red capsicum, chopped
3 small eggplants, sliced
300g tomato salsa
12 black olives

METHOD

1 Heat the oil in a frying pan and brown the pork chops.

2 Remove chops, add all the vegetables and cook until soft.

3 Add the chops, salsa and olives to the pan. Simmer on a very low heat for 1 hour. Serve with creamy mashed potato and pumpkin and a fresh green vegetable.

Hint: Lean pork cuts can be used in this recipe.

Serves 4 **Calories** 385
Fat 4.3g **Preparation** 10 mins
Cooking 1 hr 10 mins

marvellous meats

Hint: Press the mince onto the hot pan with another sheet of baking paper. This will make it easier to achieve the desired thickness for the base.

Serves 2 **Calories** 87
Fat 2.8g **Preparation** 5 mins
Cooking 15 mins

meat lover's pizza

INGREDIENTS

250g lean beef mince
sprinkle of seasoned pepper
salt to taste
2 tablespoons tomato salsa
50g Cheddar cheese, grated
sprinkle of chives, chopped
sprinkle of fresh parsley, chopped
sprinkle of ground paprika

METHOD

1 Heat an electric frying pan on high. Line with baking paper. Press the mince onto the baking paper to form base of the 'pizza'. Sprinkle with seasoned pepper and salt to taste. Cook, covered, on high until the mince changes colour. Turn the meat and continue to cook for a few minutes.

2 Place the salsa, cheese, chopped chives, parsley and paprika onto the mince and cook on medium, covered, for 5–7 minutes or until the cheese melts. Serve with vegetables as a main meal or with salad and crusty bread as a snack.

tasty
chicken

Hint: Where possible, buy your chicken free-range or corn-fed for beautiful tasting birds. You will notice the extra flavour and character of this delicately flavoured poultry.

chicken *parmigiana*

INGREDIENTS

2 teaspoons olive oil

500g crumbed chicken schnitzel

300g tomato salsa

80g low-fat cheese, grated

sprinkle of ground paprika

sprinkle of fresh parsley, chopped

sprinkle of fresh chives, chopped

Serves 4 **Calories** 369

Fat 2.3g **Preparation** 5 mins

Cooking 10 mins

METHOD

1 Line an electric frying pan with baking paper and pour some olive oil on the paper. Cook the schnitzel on high until lightly browned. Turn and spread some of the salsa on the schnitzel until covered. Sprinkle the cheese on top

2 Sprinkle the schnitzel with paprika, parsley and chives. Cover the frying pan until the cheese has melted, then serve with potato wedges and green beans.

curried *chicken*

INGREDIENTS

1 large onion, chopped

1 carrot, chopped

1 stalk celery, chopped

2 teaspoons butter

mild curry powder to taste

8 chicken drumsticks, skin removed

1–1½ cups hot water

salt and pepper to taste

½–¾ cup low-fat milk

sprinkle of fresh parsley, chopped

2 tablespoons plain flour, mixed to a paste with milk

METHOD

1 In a large frying pan, soften the vegetables in the butter, add curry powder to taste and cook for 30 seconds. Add the chicken, water and salt and pepper to taste, and simmer on a low heat for 40 minutes or until the chicken is tender.

2 Drain off some of the liquid and replace it with the low-fat milk. Bring back to a simmer, add the parsley and thicken with the flour mixture, adding it slowly and stirring until the sauce is the desired consistency. Serve with boiled rice.

Serves 4 **Calories** 460 **Fat** 8.9g

Preparation 10 mins **Cooking** 50 mins

curried chicken

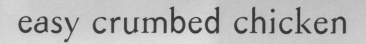

easy crumbed chicken

easy crumbed chicken

INGREDIENTS

500g chicken breast fillet
sprinkle of lemon pepper
seasoning
1 tablespoon plain flour
1 egg
½ cup dry breadcrumbs
2 tablespoons olive oil
salt to taste
juice of 1 lemon
sprinkle of fresh chives, chopped
sprinkle of fresh parsley,
chopped

Serves 4 Calories 316
Fat 2g Preparation 5 mins
Cooking 10 mins

METHOD

1 Slice the chicken breast thinly and place in a snaplock bag. Sprinkle with lemon pepper seasoning. Seal the bag and shake gently until the lemon pepper seasoning is spread evenly over the chicken.

2 Add the flour to coat the chicken and shake in the bag until it is evenly coated. Break the egg into the bag and hold the top securely as you massage the egg into the other ingredients. Now add the breadcrumbs, and once again seal the bag and shake until the chicken is coated.

3 Line an electric frying pan with baking paper and pour in the olive oil. Add the crumbed chicken and cook until it browns. Add salt to taste, turn the chicken and squeeze on some lemon juice. Add the fresh chopped chives and parsley, then cover and cook for approximately 3 minutes.

baking crumbed food

Like most children, my boys loved crispy crumbed drumsticks, golden and crunchy on the outside, tender and moist on the inside.

I've never been a big fan of high-fat food and over the years I've developed some easy alternative cooking methods.

This baking method works well for most crumbed foods, such as chicken pieces, veal or lamb, salmon rissoles and crumbed meatloaf.

Nan made her own breadcrumbs by putting any leftover bread on baking trays. These were placed in the oven to dry out in the stored heat left over from cooking the evening meal. Nothing was wasted in Nan's kitchen, not even odd bits of bread!

Hint: Why not make gourmet breadcrumbs by adding a few simple ingredients to store-bought breadcrumbs? Experiment with the following: ground paprika, chopped chives, freshly grated Parmesan cheese, mixed herbs, rosemary, oregano or parsley, chilli flakes and garlic salt, lemon pepper seasoning or lemongrass and chilli. A super breadcrumb topping is equal parts of grated Cheddar cheese and breadcrumbs, with freshly chopped chives, paprika and chilli flakes.

easy chicken stir-fry

INGREDIENTS

300g chicken breast fillets

1 tablespoon sweet chilli sauce

1 tablespoon hoisin sauce

1 tablespoon soy sauce

½ teaspoon chilli flakes

1 red capsicum, diced

1 green capsicum, diced

6 shallots, diced

1 head broccoli, separated into florets

METHOD

1 Thinly slice the chicken breast fillets. Heat a frying pan, add the sweet chilli sauce, hoisin sauce, soy sauce and chilli flakes and stir well.

2 When the sauce begins to bubble, add the chicken fillets and stir to combine. Cook for 2 minutes, then add the vegetables and stir-fry. Cover and cook for another 3 minutes, stirring regularly. Serve with boiled rice.

Serves 4 **Calories** 68

Fat 0.1g **Preparation** 5 mins

Cooking 10 mins

creamy mustard chicken

Hint: Vary this recipe with the varieties of mustards. I think the ideal is wholegrain mustard, but you can also get wholegrain honey mustard for that added sweetness. Or you might like to use German mustard, Dijon or perhaps even mild Australian or American mustard. This dish doesn't have to be high in fat, because you're only adding a little cream. I suggest using light cream and, of course, don't swamp the dish with cream – just add a couple of tablespoons.

INGREDIENTS

2 teaspoons olive oil

2 teaspoons butter

500g chicken breast fillets

sprinkle of lemon pepper seasoning

2 tablespoons plain flour

2 teaspoons wholegrain or German mustard

2 tablespoons cream

sprinkle of fresh parsley, chopped

METHOD

1 Heat the butter and olive oil on medium heat in a frying pan. Coat the chicken in lemon pepper seasoning and plain flour and add to pan. You can cook the chicken in strips or as whole breast fillets.

2 Add wholegrain or German mustard, cream and parsley to create a delicious sauce and stir frequently. Extra cream can be used in this recipe, if you want lots of sauce.

3 Serve with mashed potato and carrot and zucchini sticks. As an alternative to chicken, use veal, beef or pork strips.

Serves 4 **Calories** 192 **Fat** 3.3g **Preparation** 5 mins **Cooking** 10 mins

thai chicken meatballs

Hint: This versatile mixture can also be used as meat loaf. You will need to double the mixture. Cook at 180°C for 1 hour.

Serves 4–6 **Calories** 201
Fat 0.9g **Preparation** 10 mins
Cooking 6 mins

INGREDIENTS

500g chicken breast mince
small bunch chives, finely chopped
½ cup parsley, chopped
½ cup fresh coriander, finely chopped
2 teaspoons Thai seasoning
2cm piece fresh ginger, grated
1 egg
½ cup fresh white breadcrumbs
salt and pepper to taste
1 tablespoon cornflour
2 tablespoons peanut oil
1 teaspoon sesame oil

METHOD

1 Combine all the ingredients except the cornflour and peanut and sesame oils. Form the mixture into mini meatballs.

2 Coat meatballs with the cornflour and fry in a small amount of peanut oil with a splash of sesame oil for approximately 3 minutes on each side, until cooked through. Serve with rice and sweet chilli sauce, for dipping.

crisp chicken

INGREDIENTS

500g chicken breast fillets, cut into strips
2 tablespoons plain flour
1 egg, beaten
2 tablespoons olive oil

METHOD

1 Coat the strips of chicken in the flour first and then the egg.

2 Heat the olive oil in an electric frying pan lined with baking paper and cook the chicken until golden brown, approximately 3–5 minutes. Serve with a crisp green salad, roasted tomatoes and hot broken bread rolls.

Hint: You can vary this recipe by using fish or pork instead of chicken.

Serves 4 **Calories** 107
Fat 1.3g **Preparation** 5 mins
Cooking 5 mins

331

chicken maryland

Serves 4 **Calories** 297
Fat 2.9g **Preparation** 10 mins
Cooking 10 mins

INGREDIENTS

500g chicken breast fillets
sprinkle of lemon pepper seasoning
2 tablespoons plain flour
1–2 eggs
dry breadcrumbs
1 tablespoon olive oil
4 slices lean ham
4 slices pineapple
80g Cheddar cheese, grated
sprinkle of ground paprika
sprinkle of chives, chopped

METHOD

1 Slice the chicken fillets and coat them with lemon pepper seasoning, flour, egg and breadcrumbs.

2 Heat the olive oil in an electric frying pan lined with baking paper, add the chicken and cook until golden. Top with the ham, pineapple, cheese, ground paprika and chopped chives.

3 Cover the frying pan and allow the topping to melt. Serve with a crisp green salad and tomato wedges.

Hint: This recipe is delicious with thinly sliced chicken breast fillets, but if you don't have time buy a barbecued chicken with all the skin removed. Just combine the meat with a little garlic and butter and proceed according to the recipe. This is a simple but tasty dish that will appeal to all the family.

Fresh garlic and parsley are a must for this dish and remember to cook your pasta to al dente.

chicken pasta

INGREDIENTS

1 tablespoon butter

g chicken breast fillets, thinly sliced

1 clove garlic, crushed

small bunch chives, chopped

salt to taste

½ cup fresh parsley, finely chopped

300mL cream

sprinkle of pepper

250g penne, cooked

METHOD

1 Heat half the butter on medium heat in a frying pan. Add the chicken breast fillets, garlic, chopped chives and a little salt.

2 Cover and cook for 4 minutes, stirring occasionally. Add the remaining butter, parsley, cream, pepper and finally the hot cooked pasta. Stir through to combine. Serve in warmed bowls.

Serves 4–6 **Calories** 330

Fat 7.5g **Preparation** 10 mins **Cooking** 10 mins

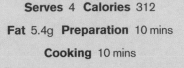

chicken supreme

Serves 4 **Calories** 312
Fat 5.4g **Preparation** 10 mins
Cooking 10 mins

INGREDIENTS

2 chicken breast fillets
80g Cheddar cheese, grated
1 bunch fresh asparagus, blanched
pepper to taste
2 tablespoons plain flour
1 egg mixed with 1 tablespoon milk
½ cup breadcrumbs to coat
a little olive oil

METHOD

1 Slice each chicken breast fillet in half to form a pocket Fill with cheese, asparagus and a sprinkle of pepper. Close each breast with toothpicks and coat with the flour egg mixture and breadcrumbs in turn.

2 In an electric frying pan lined with baking paper, add the olive oil and cook the chicken breasts until golden brown. Turn and repeat. Approximately 4–5 minutes on each side is enough. Serve with watercress, asparagus and green beans.

sensational
seafood

brenda's famous red salmon dip

Serves 6 **Calories** 258

Fat 2.85g **Preparation** 10 mins

INGREDIENTS

210g canned red salmon

sprinkle of lemon pepper seasoning

sprinkle of ground paprika

250g cream cheese

½ bunch chives, chopped

squeeze of fresh lemon juice

METHOD

1 Mix all ingredients together well. Serve with fresh chilled crudités, such as celery, carrots and cauliflower, all cut into bite-sized pieces.

italian *prawns*

INGREDIENTS

1 tablespoon olive oil

1 teaspoon butter

1 small onion, finely chopped

4 cloves garlic, crushed

2 rashers very lean bacon, finely chopped

sprinkle of chilli flakes

400g canned chopped tomatoes

400g green prawns, peeled and deveined

salt and pepper to taste

1 teaspoon ground paprika

pinch of sugar

fresh parsley to garnish

METHOD

1 Heat the olive oil and butter over a high heat in an electric frying pan. Add the onion, garlic, bacon and chilli flakes. Cook until softened, for about 5 minutes.

2 Add the can of tomatoes, lower the heat and simmer for 30 minutes, uncovered, to reduce the sauce.

3 Add the prawns and cook only until they change colour, turning heat up to medium. Season to taste and add paprika and sugar. Serve in individual bowls with crusty bread, garnished with parsley, or stir through hot cooked pasta as a main course.

Serves 4 **Calories** 91 **Fat** 0.95g **Preparation** 10 mins **Cooking** 40 mins

whole thai fish

Serves 4 **Calories** 615
Fat 1.6g **Preparation** 10 mins
Cooking 30 mins

INGREDIENTS

4 whole fish

sprinkle of lemon pepper seasoning

1 tablespoon plain flour

2 tablespoons olive oil

300g sweet chilli sauce

salt and pepper to taste

METHOD

1 Cut or score 3 openings on each side of the fish to allow the flavours to penetrate. Sprinkle with lemon pepper seasoning and coat with the plain flour.

2 Heat the olive oil in a frying pan. Add the fish (2 at a time) and cook for 5 minutes.

3 Turn the fish and coat with sweet chilli sauce, seasoning while cooking, then cook for a further 8 minutes or until the fish flakes easily. Serve on a bed of jasmine rice, garnished with sliced cucumber, shallots and fresh chopped coriander.

master soy fish

INGREDIENTS

500g boneless ocean trout fillets,
1 tablespoon olive oil
sprinkle of soy sauce
salt and pepper to taste
shallots, chopped to serve

METHOD

1 Heat the olive oil in a frying pan. Add the fish fillets and sprinkle a little soy sauce and seasoning on each fillet.

2 Cover and cook for 2 minutes, turn and repeat.

3 Serve on a bed of steamed jasmine rice with bok choy, garnished with shallots.

Hint: You can use either ocean trout or fresh salmon steak-style cuts as a fool-proof alternative when frying.

Serves 4 **Calories** 497
Fat 1.6g **Preparation** 5 mins
Cooking 5 mins

339

Hint: To reduce the amount of salt in this dish you may like to soak the smoked fish in water for a short while before cooking.

Serves 4 **Calories** 250
Fat 2.2g **Preparation** 5 mins
Cooking 10 mins

saucy smoked fish

INGREDIENTS

500g smoked fish
2 teaspoons butter
¾ cup milk
¼ teaspoon ground nutmeg
salt and pepper
1 tablespoon plain flour mixed to a paste with 2 tablespoons of milk
¼ cup fresh parsley, chopped

METHOD

1 Place the fish in a microwave-safe dish. Add the butter and the milk. Poach the fish in the microwave on medium-high heat for 3–5 minutes or until the fish flakes easily.

2 Remove the fish from the liquid and set aside. Place nutmeg and salt and pepper in the fish cooking liquid, and stir in the flour and milk mixture.

3 Reheat the sauce in the microwave on high for 2 minutes, stirring every 30 seconds or until the sauce thickens. Place the fish on plates and spoon over the sauce. Serve with lightly steamed sliced carrots, peas and corn and garnish with parsley.

seafood soup

INGREDIENTS

2 medium onions, chopped

2 cloves garlic, chopped

2 teaspoons butter

400g canned chopped tomatoes

1 cup fresh, raw seafood such as prawns, fish, oysters and mussels

sprinkle of chilli powder

salt and pepper to taste

¼ cup fresh parsley, chopped

small bunch fresh chives, chopped

METHOD

1 Soften the onion and garlic in the melted butter in a large saucepan, add the chopped tomatoes and bring to the boil. Simmer for 5 minutes. Add the seafood and simmer for a further 5 minutes.

2 Add the seasonings, parsley and chives. Serve in warmed bowls with crusty bread.

341

Serves 4 **Calories** 180 **Fat** 1.6g **Preparation** 10 mins **Cooking** 10 mins

prawn omelette

Serves 4 **Calories** 342
Fat 1.8g **Preparation** 5 mins
Cooking 10 mins

INGREDIENTS

4 large eggs
250g cooked prawns, peeled
and deveined
75g cabbage, shredded
1 small onion, finely sliced
1 cup bean sprouts
4 shallots, chopped
2 tablespoons water
1 carrot, grated
1 teaspoon olive oil
salt and pepper

METHOD

1 Combine all the ingredients except the olive oil and salt and pepper.

2 Heat an electric frying pan on high, then line with baking paper. Drizzle in the olive oil.

3 Pour in the omelette mixture on top of the paper and cook, covered, until set. Cut into 4 portions and turn each portion over. Season to taste. Cover and cook for a further 2 minutes.

easy
vegetables

easy vegetables

noodle salad

INGREDIENTS

300g red, savoy or Chinese cabbage, shredded

1 tablespoon soy sauce

1 red capsicum, finely sliced

2 tablespoons honey

4 shallots, chopped

60mL Italian dressing

100g Chinese fried noodles

sprinkle of fresh chilli, chopped

½ cup slivered almonds, toasted

METHOD

1 Combine all the ingredients and enjoy this fabulous salad.

Serves 4–6 **Calories** 259

Fat 1.9g **Preparation** 10 mins

brenda's brilliant rice salad

INGREDIENTS

1 large onion, chopped

1 cup frozen peas

1 cup frozen corn kernels

2 tablespoons butter

4 cups cooked jasmine rice

4 cloves garlic, crushed

6 large cooked prawns, peeled and deveined

2 tablespoons olive oil

juice of 1 lemon

3 eggs beaten with 2 tablespoons fresh chives, chopped

sprinkle of mild curry powder

sprinkle of pepper steak seasoning

2 slices lean ham, chopped

¼ cup fresh chives, chopped

METHOD

1 Combine the onion, peas and corn and cook in the microwave for 3 minutes in a covered container with 1 tablespoon of the butter. Stir into the cooked jasmine rice.

2 Melt half of the remaining butter in a frying pan and cook the crushed garlic until soft. Add the prawns to heat through, then add the mixture to the rice with the olive oil and lemon juice.

3 Place the egg mixture into the frying pan and cook in the remaining butter. When cooked, cut into thin strips and add to the rice, with the mild curry powder and the pepper steak seasoning. Toss to combine, add ham and sprinkle with fresh chives.

Serves 4–6 **Calories** 297

Fat 4.1g **Preparation** 15 mins

Cooking 10 mins

345

famous mushroom pizza

famous mushroom pizza

INGREDIENTS

base
1 sachet dry yeast
1 cup warm water
1 teaspoon sugar
3 tablespoons olive oil
1 teaspoon salt
3 cups plain flour, sifted

topping
2 tablespoons olive oil
300g tomato salsa
1 onion, sliced
50g mushrooms, sliced
50g Mozzarella cheese, grated
salt and pepper to taste
sprinkle of oregano leaves

METHOD

1 Dissolve the yeast in the warm water with the sugar. Let stand until it foams. Add the yeast mixture, olive oil and salt to the flour. Mix to combine and set aside until doubled in size.

2 Turn out onto a floured board and knead to form a soft dough.

3 Press a piece of the dough about the size of a tennis ball onto a pizza tray. You could use a cone tray or even a large baking dish.

4 Preheat the oven to 225°C. Brush the pizza base with 1 tablespoon of olive oil, spread liberally with salsa, then add the onion and mushrooms. Drizzle with more olive oil and cover liberally with the cheese, salt and pepper to taste. Sprinkle with the oregano leaves. Bake for 20 minutes.

the girls and the babies

Ten girls and ten babies! We met during our pre-natal classes at the local health clinic. Our first meeting after the birth of our babies was at my place!

This was my second child, but for everyone else it was their first. During our last class, something told me that supporting each other after the big events would be a great idea.

As the big day approached, my thoughts turned to food and to making our first gathering something really special. I wanted my dish to be spectacular! With its pizza base, home-made of course, topped with a tasty tomato salsa, onions, mushrooms and grated cheese and baked to golden perfection in a hot oven – was a real winner!

Hint: For the best flavour, use large field mushrooms, peeled and thinly sliced. Making your own pizza base is well worth the extra time and effort. Pizza dough can be frozen and used later.

347

Serves 4 **Calories** 496 **Fat** 6.8g **Preparation** 10 mins **Cooking** 20–25 mins

easy vegetables

Hint: Use the all-purpose cheese topping as a topping for deli hashbrowns, or mix a little of the topping through scrambled eggs. Alternatively, stuff mushroom caps with the topping and cook in the microwave until the cheese melts. It can also be used as a pizza topping, grilled on muffins or toast, or as a filling for an omelette. Place a little on top of cooked rissoles or chicken or veal schnitzel.

all-purpose cheese topping

INGREDIENTS
500g Cheddar cheese, grated
sprinkle of ground paprika
small bunch chives, chopped
¼ cup fresh parsley, chopped
sprinkle of pepper
1 red capsicum, finely chopped
optional ingredients
bacon, onion and ham, all finely chopped

Serves 8 **Calories** 204
Fat 5.2g **Preparation** 10 mins

METHOD
1 Mix all ingredients together and freeze in a snaplock bag or refrigerate until ready to use.

fresh salsa

INGREDIENTS
1 baguette, sliced
2 teaspoons garlic bread seasoning
8 Roma tomatoes, finely chopped
1 medium red onion, finely chopped
¼ cup fresh basil, chopped
salt to taste
1 tablespoon olive oil
30mL balsamic vinegar

Serves 8 **Calories** 98 **Fat** 1g
Preparation 10 mins

METHOD
1 In a bowl, combine all ingredients, except for the bread

2 Spread sliced crusty bread with butter and a sprinkle of garlic bread seasoning. Grill or bake until golden brown.

3 Serve the fresh salsa on hot garlic bread. This salsa is good if prepared a few hours in advance.

extravagent
eggs

extravagent eggs

Hint: Using a sharp knife, cut a small piece of ham from the centre of the hamsteak. Don't cut through the hamsteak – rather, try to create a small area to hold in the egg.

Hint: Finely chop ingredients such as capsicum, mushrooms, shallots or cabbage before incorporating into the omelette mixture. Also grate the cheese. It will help to disperse all of the flavours.

easy ham and eggs

INGREDIENTS

1 hamsteak
1 egg
25g Cheddar cheese, grated
sprinkle of ground paprika
¼ cup fresh parsley, chopped
small bunch chives, chopped

Serves 1 **Calories** 214
Fat 3.5g **Preparation** 5 mins
Cooking 2 mins

METHOD

1 Place a sheet of baking paper on a saucer. On top of this put the hamsteak and break the egg onto it. Try to manoeuvre the yolk to the middle of the hamsteak and have the egg white cover the rest until it partially flows o the edge.

2 The rounded base of the saucer will help hold the sha of the egg. Pierce the yolk and sprinkle a little grated cheese onto the egg, then sprinkle with paprika, parsle and chives.

3 Cover the saucer, put into a microwave and cook on h for 1½ minutes or until the egg is the way you like it.

easy perfect omelette

INGREDIENTS

4 large eggs
1 tablespoon thickened cream
¾ cup all-purpose cheese topping (page 46)
salt and pepper to taste

METHOD

1 Gently beat together all the ingredients in a small bow

2 Turn an electric frying pan to high and line with bakin paper. Pour egg mixture into frying pan, cover, and cook on full power until set. This will take about 5 minutes. To turn the omelette, take two corners of the baking paper and pull to one side and your omelette will fold in half perfectly. Serve with a little rocket.

Serves 2 **Calories** 268.5 **Fat** 13g **Preparation** 5 mins **Cooking** 5 mins

easy perfect omelette

extravagent eggs

toad in the hole

Serves 4 **Calories** 148

Fat 2.9g **Preparation** 5 mins

Cooking 5 mins

INGREDIENTS

a little soft butter

4 slices bread, with a hole the size of a 50-cent piece cut out of the centre

4 eggs

salt and pepper to taste

¼ cup fresh chives, chopped

METHOD

1 Heat an electric frying pan on high, then line with a sheet of baking paper. Butter the bread and place buttered side down in a heated frying pan. Cook until golden brown.

2 Turn over and break an egg into the hole in each slice of bread. Season with pepper and salt to taste, cover and cook until the egg is set. Sprinkle with a little chopped fresh chives before serving. Turn again for a well done egg.

delicious
desserts

Hint: Store left over fruit in a snaplock bag to prevent it discolouring.

granny's apple pancakes

INGREDIENTS

4 Granny Smith apples, peeled and thinly sliced
2 tablespoons butter
2 tablespoons brown sugar
sprinkle of mixed spice
½ cup sultanas
375g pancake mix
icing sugar

Serves 6 Calories 279
Fat 2.8g Preparation 5 mins
Cooking 10 mins

METHOD

1 In an electric frying pan lined with baking paper, sauté thinly sliced apples in butter and brown sugar until soft. Add a sprinkle of mixed spice and sultanas.

2 Pour pancake mix over the fruit. Place the lid on the pan and cook until firm. Sprinkle with icing sugar, cut into slices and serve with ice cream, custard or cream. Serve upside-down to display the beautiful glazed fruit.

Hint: For extra flavour, add fresh passionfruit after cooking.

rhubarb and apple

INGREDIENTS

1 bunch rhubarb, stems only, washed and chopped
2 Granny Smith apples, peeled and sliced
½ cup sugar
¾ cup water
sprinkle of ground nutmeg

METHOD

1 Place the rhubarb and apples into a large microwave-safe bowl. Add the sugar and water.

2 Cook, uncovered, in a microwave on high for 15 minutes, stirring every 5 minutes.

3 Sprinkle a little ground nutmeg over the fruit mixture. Serve with cream, custard or ice cream.

Serves 4 Calories 155 Fat 0.1g Preparation 10 mins Cooking 15 mins

rhubarb and apple

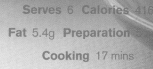

fruity pan scones

Hint: By using an electric frying pan to cook these scones you avoid having to use your oven.

A frying pan is far more economical.

Remember:

1 scone = 15 seconds

2 scones = 25 seconds

Fruity pan scones are ideal for camping or caravaning.

INGREDIENTS

1 cup sultanas

3 cups self-raising flour, sifted

1 cup milk

1 cup thickened cream

a little extra flour

METHOD

1 Add the sultanas to the flour, then add the milk and cream. Using a knife, stir to make a sticky dough.

2 Turn the mixture out onto a floured board, sprinkle with a little extra flour and pat into a rectangular shape, approximately 3cm high.

3 Cut out scones with a scone cutter. Place scones in an electric frying pan lined with baking paper. Cook, covered, on medium for 5 minutes.

4 Turn scones and cook for a further 5–8 minutes. Serve with jam and cream. The scones can also be cooked in a conventional oven, preheated to 220°C, for 15 minutes.

Serves 6 Calories 416

Fat 5.4g Preparation 9 mins

Cooking 17 mins

fabulous fruit salad

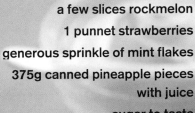

INGREDIENTS

1 peach
1 green apple
1 red apple
1 mango
a few slices rockmelon
1 punnet strawberries
generous sprinkle of mint flakes
375g canned pineapple pieces
with juice
sugar to taste

METHOD

1 Dice all the fruit ingredients except the pineapple, and gently mix together in a bowl.

2 Add the mint flakes and the pineapple pieces with juice. Gently stir through.

3 Dust the fruit salad lightly with sugar. Refrigerate until cool.

Serves 4 **Calories** 78.6g
Fat 0.1g **Preparation** 5 mins

357

banana *surprise*

INGREDIENTS

2 tablespoons honey

2 tablespoons butter

sprinkle of ground nutmeg

2 firm bananas, sliced into chunks

sprinkle of ground cinnamon

METHOD

1 Place the honey and butter into a microwave-safe scontainer. Sprinkle the ground nutmeg over the top and heat in a microwave for 30 seconds on high.

2 Gently stir the bananas through the warm honey mixture and cook on high for 30 seconds to warm. Sprinkle with a little ground cinnamon. Serve with ice cream, cream or sour cream.

Serves 4 **Calories** 202

Fat 3.8g **Preparation** 5 mins

Cooking 1 min

banana pancakes

INGREDIENTS

2 tablespoons butter

2 cups pancake mix or 375g shaker pack

2 medium bananas, sliced

¼ cup cinnamon sugar

1⅓ cups golden syrup

6 small scoop ice cream

METHOD

1 Combine the pancake batter and sliced bananas.

2 Heat the butter in a frying pan and cook the pancake mixture in butter in the pan until bubbles appear on the surface. Turn and cook until golden in colour.

3 Serve each portion with a good sprinkle of cinnamon sugar, golden syrup, and a scoop of ice cream.

Serves 6 **Calories** 257
Fat 9.2g **Preparation** 5 mins
Cooking 6 mins

Hint: This cake cuts well if prepared the day before it is required.

forest berry magic

INGREDIENTS

1 good quality chocolate cake mix

small quantity of liqueur, optional

1 punnet fresh strawberries, or other berries in season

750mL cream, whipped

dark chocolate, grated

METHOD

1 Prepare the cake mix, using a fork to mix the ingredients, but do not over-beat.

2 Cut out three circles of baking paper the size of a dinner plate and place each circle onto a plate.

3 Put a third of the cake mix onto each plate circle and cook each individually on high in the microwave for 3–4 minutes. Allow to cool.

4 Select one cake, invert it, and remove the baking paper. Sprinkle with liqueur if desired, and top with some the fruit and whipped cream.

5 Place the second cake on top of the first, and repeat. Finally, add the third layer, then cover the entire cake with the remaining cream. Top with a little fruit and the grated dark chocolate.

6 Place a large bowl over the cake and refrigerate overnight. Make sure the bowl does not touch the cake top.

Serves 6–8 **Calories** 324

Fat 10.5g **Preparation** 5 mins

Cooking 10 mins

blueberry soft-bake cookies

INGREDIENTS

150g plain flour

1½ teaspoons baking powder

½ teaspoon cinnamon

55g butter, cubed, plus extra for greasing

85g caster sugar

100mL milk

150g fresh blueberries

METHOD

1 Preheat the oven to 190°C. Grease a large baking tray. Sift the flour, baking powder and cinnamon into a bowl. Rub in the butter, using your fingertips, until the mixture resembles breadcrumbs, then stir in the sugar.

2 Stir in the milk and blueberries until just combined – the dough should be sticky. Spoon 8 mounds, spaced well apart, onto the baking tray and cook for 20 minutes or until golden. Cool on a wire rack for a few minutes before serving.

Hint: If you fancy a change, try using a few chopped strawberries instead of the blueberries. You can also substitute your favourite chocolate for some of the berry quantity. My boys love these made with two-thirds blueberry and one-third white chocolate. These are a delicious muffin-type biscuit and are best eaten hot.

Serves 4 **Calories** 313
Fat 9.6g **Preparation** 10 mins
Cooking 20 mins

basic tomato sauce

INGREDIENTS

2 cloves garlic, crushed
2 tablespoons olive oil
400g chopped Roma tomatoes
10 leaves fresh basil, chopped
sprinkle of sea salt
sprinkle of cracked black peppercorns

METHOD

1 Gently fry the crushed garlic in the olive oil until it softens. Add the rest of the ingredients and simmer, uncovered, until reduced to half the quantity. Serve with freshly cooked pasta, vegetarian lasagne, cooked crumbed meat, fish or chicken. Top with grated Cheddar cheese and grill until golden brown.

Serves 4   Calories 354   Fat 3.8g   Preparation 5 mins   Cooking 10 mins

curry mayonnaise

INGREDIENTS

½ cup whole-egg mayonnaise
¼ cup fresh parsley, finely chopped
½ teaspoon curry powder
squeeze of fresh lime juice

METHOD

1 Mix all ingredients together. Serve with poached salmon, steamed chicken breast, cooked prawns on a bed of rocket and Mesclun salad, fresh oysters, pasta with smoked salmon or Danish open sandwiches of chicken or salmon.

Serves 4   Calories 470   Fat 5.8g   Preparation 5 min

mushroom sauce

INGREDIENTS

2 teaspoons butter
1 clove garlic, crushed
250g flat mushrooms, chopped
salt and pepper to taste
2 teaspoons plain flour
small bunch chives, chopped
3 tablespoons skim milk

METHOD

1 Heat the butter in a frying pan over a medium heat, add the garlic, mushrooms, salt and pepper.

2 Cover and cook for a few minutes until the mushroom soften but are still firm. Sprinkle the flour over the mushrooms and blend with a fork, then add the chives. Blend in the milk to create a smooth sauce. Reduce hea and simmer for 1–2 minutes.

3 Serve on hot toasted sourdough bread or crusty brea

Serves 4   Calories 165   Fat 5g   Preparation 5 mins   Cooking 5 mins

glossary

al dente: an Italian cooking term for ingredients that are cooked until tender but still firm to the bite; usually applied to pasta.

balsamic vinegar: a mild, extremely fragrant, wine-based vinegar made in northern Italy. Traditionally, the vinegar is aged for at least 7 years in a series of casks made of various woods.

baste: to moisten food while it is cooking by spooning or brushing on liquid or fat.

bain marie: a saucepan standing in a large pan which is filled with boiling water to keep liquids at simmering point. A double boiler will do the same job.

beat: to stir thoroughly and vigorously.

blanch: to plunge into boiling water and then, in some cases, into cold water. Fruits and nuts are blanched to remove skin easily.

blend: to mix thoroughly.

brown: to cook in a small amount of fat until brown.

butter: to spread with softened or melted butter.

butterfly: to slit a piece of food in half horizontally, cutting it almost through so that when opened it resembles butterfly wings. Chops, large prawns and thick fish fillets are often butterflied so that they cook more quickly.

caramelise: to melt sugar until it is a golden-brown syrup.

champignons: small mushrooms, usually canned.

coat: to cover with a thin layer of flour, sugar, nuts, crumbs, poppy or sesame seeds, cinnamon sugar or a few of the ground spices.

cream: to make soft, smooth and creamy by rubbing with back of spoon or by beating with a mixer. Usually applied to fat and sugar.

croutons: small toasted or fried cubes of bread.

crudités: raw vegetables, whether cut in slices or sticks to nibble plain or with a dipping sauce, or shredded and tossed as salad with a simple dressing.

cube: to cut into small pieces with six equal sides.

curdle: to cause milk or sauce to separate into solid and liquid. An example, overcooked egg mixtures.

deglaze: to dissolve congealed cooking juices or glaze on the bottom of a pan by adding a liquid, then scraping and stirring vigorously whilst bringing the liquid to the boil. Juices may be used to make gravy or to add to sauce.

devilled: a dish or sauce that is highly seasoned with a hot ingredient such as mustard, worcestershire sauce or cayenne pepper.

dice: to cut into small cubes.

dietary fibre: a plant-cell material that is undigested or only partially digested in the human body but which promotes healthy digestion of other food matter.

dissolve: mix a dry ingredient with liquid until absorbed.

drizzle: to pour in a fine thread-like stream over a surface.

dust: to sprinkle or coat lightly with flour or icing sugar.

entrée: in Europe, the 'entry' or hors d'oeuvre; in North America, the main course.

fillet: a special cut of beef, lamb, pork or veal; breast of poultry and game; fish cut off the bone lengthwise.

flake: to break into small pieces with a fork.

flame: to ignite warmed alcohol over food.

fold in: a gentle, careful combining of a light or delicate mixture with a heavier mixture using a metal spoon.

garnish: to decorate food, usually with something edible.

glaze: a thin coating of beaten egg, syrup or aspic which is brushed over pastry, fruits or cooked meats.

gratin: a dish cooked in the oven or under the grill so that it develops a brown crust. Breadcrumbs or cheese may be sprinkled on top first. Shallow gratin dishes ensure a maximum area of crust.

grease: to rub or brush lightly with oil or fat.

joint: to cut poultry, game or small animals into serving pieces by dividing at the joint.

julienne: to cut food into match-like strips.

knead: to work dough using heel of hand with a pressing motion, while stretching and folding the dough.

line: to cover the inside of a container with paper, to protect or aid in removing mixture.

marinade: a seasoned liquid, usually an oil and acid mixture, in which meats or other foods are soaked to soften and give more flavour.

marinate: to let food stand in a marinade to season and tenderise.

melt: to heat until liquified.

mince: to grind into very small pieces.

mix: to combine ingredients by stirring.

olive oil: various grades of oil extract from olives. Extra virgin olive oil has a full, fruity flavour and the lowest acidity. Virgin olive oil is slightly higher in acidity and lighter in flavour. Pure olive oil is a processed blend of olive oils and has the highest acidity and lightest taste.

peel: to strip away outside covering.

poach: to simmer gently in enough hot liquid to cover, using care to retain shape of food.

purée: a smooth paste, usually of vegetables or fruits, made by putting foods through a sieve, food mill or liquefying in a blender or food processor.

reduce: to cook over a very high heat, uncovered, until the liquid is reduced by evaporation.

rubbing-in: a method of incorporating fat into flour, by use of fingertips only. Also incorporates air into mixture.

salsa: a juice derived from the main ingredient being cooked or a sauce added to a dish to enhance its flavour. In Italy the term is often used for pasta sauces; in Mexico the name usually applies to uncooked sauces served as an accompaniment, especially to corn chips.

sauté: to cook or brown in small amount of hot fat.

score: to mark food with cuts, notches of lines to prevent curling or to make food more attractive.

scald: to bring just to boiling point, usually for milk. Also to rinse with boiling water.

sear: to brown surface quickly over high heat.

seasoned flour: flour with salt and pepper added.

sift: to shake a dry, powdered substance through a sieve or sifter to remove any lumps and give lightness.

simmer: to cook food gently in liquid that bubbles steadily just below boiling point so that the food cooks in even heat without breaking up.

skim: to remove a surface layer (often of impurities and scum) from a liquid with a metal spoon or small ladle.

slivered: sliced in long, thin pieces. Usually refers to nuts, especially almonds.

stir-fry: to cook thin slices of meat and vegetable over a high heat in a small amount of oil, stirring constantly cook evenly in a short time. Traditionally done in a wok; however, a heavy based frying pan may be used.

stock: a liquid containing flavours, extracts and nutrients of bones, meat, fish or vegetables.

thicken: to thicken a hot liquid by stirring a thin, smooth paste of arrowroot, cornflour or flour with an equal amount of cold water until thickened.

toss: to gently mix ingredients with two forks or fork and spoon.

whip: to beat rapidly, incorporate air and produce expansion.

zest: thin outer layer of citrus fruits containing the aromatic citrus oil. It is usually thinly pared with a vegetable peeler or grated with a zester or grater to separate it from the bitter white pith underneath.

363

weights and *measures*

Cooking is not an exact science: one does not require finely calibrated scales, pipettes and scientific equipment to cook, yet the conversion to metric measures in some countries and its interpretations must have intimidated many a good cook.

Weights are given in the recipes only for ingredients such as meats, fish, poultry and some vegetables. Remember, however, that a few grams/ounces one way or the other will not affect the success of your dish.

Although recipes have been tested using the Australian Standard 250mL cup, 20mL tablespoon and 5mL teaspoon, they will work just as well with the US and Canadian 8fl oz cup, or the UK 300mL cup. We have used graduated cup measures in preference to tablespoon measures so that proportions are always the same. Where tablespoon measures have been given, these are not crucial measures, so using the smaller tablespoon of the US or UK will not affect the recipe's success. At least we all agree on the teaspoon size.

For breads, cakes and pastries, the only area which might cause concern is where eggs are used, as proportions will then vary. If working with a 250mL or 300mL cup, use large eggs (65g/2^1/4 oz), adding a little more liquid to the recipe for 300mL cup measures if it seems necessary. Use the medium-sized eggs (55g/2 oz) with 8fl oz cup measure. A graduated set of measuring cups and spoons is recommended, the cups in particular for measuring dry ingredients. Remember to level such ingredients to ensure their accuracy.

English Measures

All measurements are similar to Australian with two exceptions: the English cup measures 300mL/10fl oz, whereas the Australian cup measures 250mL/8^3/4fl oz. The English tablespoon (the Australian dessertspoon) measures 14.8mL/^{1}/2 fl oz against the Australian tablespoon of 20mL/^{2}/3 fl oz.

The Imperial measurement is 20fl oz to the pint, 40fl oz a quart and 160fl oz one gallon.

American Measures

The American reputed pint is 16fl oz, a quart is equal to 32fl oz, the American gallon, 128fl oz. The American tablespoon is equal to 14.8mL/^{1}/2 fl oz, and the teaspoon is 5mL/^{1}/6 fl oz. The cup measure is 250mL/8^3/4fl oz, the same as in Australia.

Dry Measures

All the measures are level, so when you have filled a cup or spoon, level it off with the edge of a knife. The scale opposite is the 'cook's equivalent'; it is not an exact conversion of metric to imperial measurement. To calculate the exact metric equivalent yourself, multiply ounces by 28.349523 to obtain grams, or divide grams by 28.349523 to obtain ounces.

Metric	Imperial
g = grams	oz = ounces
kg = kilograms	lb = pounds
15g	^{1}/2oz
20g	^{2}/3oz
30g	1oz
55g	2oz
85g	3oz
115g	4oz/^{1}/4 lb
145g	5oz
170g	6oz
200g	7oz
225g	8oz/^{1}/2 lb
255g	9oz
285g	10oz
310g	11oz
340g	12oz/^{3}/4 lb
370g	13oz
400g	14oz
425g	15oz
1kg	1lb/35.2oz/2.2 lb
1.5kg	3.3 lb

weights and *measures*

Oven Temperatures

The Celsius temperatures given here are not exact; they have been rounded off and are given as a guide only. Follow the manufacturer's temperature guide, relating it to oven description given in the recipe. Remember gas ovens are hottest at the top, electric ovens at the bottom and convection-fan forced ovens are usually even throughout. We included Regulo numbers for gas cookers, which may assist. To convert °C to °F multiply °C by 9, divide by 5, then add 32.

Oven Temperatures

	C°	F°	Regular
Very slow	120	250	1
Slow	150	300	2
Moderately slow	160	325	3
Moderate	180	350	4
Moderately hot	190–200	370–400	5–6
Hot	210–220	410–440	6–7
Very hot	230	450	8
Super hot	250–290	475–500	9–10

Cake Dish Sizes

Metric	Imperial
15cm	6in
18cm	7in
20cm	8in
23cm	9in

Loaf Dish Sizes

Metric	Imperial
23x12cm	9x5in
25x8cm	10x3in
28x18cm	11x7in

Liquid Measures

Metric	Imperial	Cup and Spoon
millilitres	fluid ounce	
5mL	1/6 fl oz	1 teaspoon
18mL	1/2 fl oz	1 dessertspoon
20mL	2/3 fl oz	1 tablespoon
30mL	1fl oz	(1 tablespoon plus 2 teaspoons)

55mL	2fl oz	
62mL	2¹/6fl oz	1/4 cup
85mL	3fl oz	1/3 cup
115mL	4fl oz	
125mL	4¹/2fl oz	1/2 cup
150mL	5¹/4fl oz	
185mL	6¹/2fl oz	3/4 cup
225mL	8fl oz	
250mL	8³/4fl oz	1 cup
285mL	10fl oz	
340mL	12fl oz	
375mL	13fl oz	1¹/2 cups
400mL	14fl oz	
435mL	15¹/3fl oz	1³/4 cups
455mL	16fl oz	
500mL	17¹/2fl oz	2 cups
567mL	20fl oz	1 pint
625mL	22fl oz	2¹/2 cups
1 litre	35fl oz	4 cups

Cup Measurements

One cup is equal to the following weights.

	Metric	Imperial
Almonds, flaked	90g	3oz
Almonds, slivered, ground	115g	4oz
Almonds, kernel	145g	5oz
Apples, dried, chopped	115g	4oz
Apricots, dried, chopped	170g	6oz
Breadcrumbs, packet	115g	4oz
Breadcrumbs, soft	55g	2oz
Cheese, grated	115g	4oz
Choc bits	145g	5oz
Coconut, desiccated	85g	3oz
Cornflakes	30g	1oz
Currants	145g	5oz
Flour	115g	4oz
Fruit, dried (mixed, sultanas etc)	170g	6oz
Ginger, crystallised, glace	225g	8oz
Honey, treacle, Golden syrup	285g	10oz
Mixed peel	200g	7oz
Nuts, chopped	115g	4oz
Prunes, chopped	200g	7oz
Rice, cooked	145g	5oz
Rice, uncooked	200g	7oz
Rolled oats	85g	3oz
Sesame seeds	115g	4oz
Shortening (butter, margarine)	225g	8oz
Sugar, brown	145g	5oz
Sugar, granulated or caster	225g	8oz
Sugar, sifted icing	145g	5oz
Wheatgerm	55g	2oz

Length

Some of us still have trouble converting imperial length to metric. In this scale, measures have been rounded off to the easiest to use and most acceptable figures. To obtain the exact metric equivalent in converting inches to centimetres, multiply inches by 2.54 whereby 1 inch equals 25.4 millimetres and 1 millimetre equals 0.03937 inches.

mm = millimetres   in = inches
cm = centimetres   ft = feet

5mm, 0.5cm	1/4 in
10mm, 1.0cm	1/2 in
20mm, 2.0cm	3/4 in
2¹/2cm	1in
5cm	2in
7¹/2cm	3in
10cm	4in
12¹/2cm	5in
15cm	6in
18cm	7in
20cm	8in
23cm	9in
25cm	10in
28cm	11in
30cm	12in (1ft)

index

all-purpose cheese topping	348	celery bites	94	chorizo, potato and dill wrap	296
antipasto skewers	116	cheese-topped ravioli	54	cocktail chicken soy and linseed baskets	101
apple muffins	174	cheese and garlic baguette	234	cocktail pumpkin and spinach pastries	75
apricot balls	174	cheese and olive wrap	250	continental frankfurter special	217
asian chicken wrap	264	cheesy meatballs	155	corned beef and potato wrap	297
aussie burger wrap	294	cheesy salmon patties	32	corned beef hash	56
bacon, avocado and cheese melt	190	cheesy scrambled eggs	130	creamy chicken pasta	333
bacon, tomato and cheese melt	192	chicken, asparagus and fetta wrap	262	creamy mustard chicken	329
bacon and egg melt	190	chicken and asparagus melt	202	creamy pepper steak	314
baked bean muffin	130	chicken and asparagus rolls	92	creamy prawn wrap	272
baked chicken and mushroom crepes	48	chicken and corn melt	202	creamy scrambled eggs	10
baked meatballs	57	chicken and ham fritters	44	crisp chicken	331
balsamic beef melt	212	chicken and mushroom melt	204	crisp chicken tortillas	145
banana and pancetta melt	193	chicken and noodles with green sauce	144	crispy bacon melt	195
banana pancakes	359	chicken and salad wrap	142	crispy chicken fingers	98
banana surprise	358	chicken and spinach delight	205	crispy fish tortilla	277
barbecue baby octopus	82	chicken and vegetable slice	52	crispy zucchini slices	73
basic pie filling	317	chicken caesar wrap	250	crumbed button mushrooms	70
basic tomato sauce	362	chicken croquette salad	47	crumbed camembert wedges	72
beef wraps	302	chicken maryland	332	crunchy granola	132
best bikkies	176	chicken nibbles	142	crustless chicken, pumpkin and spinach pie	46
blueberry soft-bake cookies	361	chicken parmigiana	324	curried chicken	324
bolognese melt	212	chicken pesto melt	206	curried egg rolls	70
breakfast feast	13	chicken supreme	334	curry mayonnaise	362
breakfast mushrooms	22	chicken swiss melt	207	curry yoghurt cutlets	114
brenda's brilliant rice salad	345	chicken tandoori skewers	95	deli and vegie sensation	286
brenda's famous red salmon dip	336	chicken waldorf salad wrap	260	deli chicken, mushroom and almond wrap	299
brenda's irish stew	310	chilli con carne	310	deli flavour melt	236
brie, ham and avocado wrap	284	chinese pork fillet	104	dips and sticks	164
bruschetta varieties	22	chipolatas, beans and corn chips	152	easy bacon pizza	10
caprese salad	24	chocolate cookies	177	easy cheesy nuggets	14

asy chicken bake	147	home-made burgers	154	mexican stuffed bun	199
asy chicken stir-fry	328	honey mustard chicken drumettes	92	mighty mini muffins	137
asy crumbed chicken	327	honey soy chicken wrap	265	mini dill balls	119
asy ham and eggs	350	hot toasted sausage wrap	294	mini flatbread pizza	166
asy perfect omelette	350	hunza chicken bake	49	mini frittatas	76
gg and smoked bacon tarts	104	individual corn chip bake	120	mini fruit salad in an orange basket	181
gg in a nest	12	italian deli wrap	288	mini meatloaves	158
ggs in pots	10	italian flavours	214	mini meaty balls	319
bulous fruit salad	357	italian prawns	337	mini penne with chicken, cheese	
bulous pan frittata	16	italian tartlets	107	and tomato sauce	149
mous chicken sesame burgers	44	jeff's special poached eggs	135	moroccan lamb meatballs	121
mous mushroom pizza	347	kind of kedgeree	34	moroccan lamb salad wraps	318
tta, olive and oregano muffins	25	lamb's fry and bacon	59	moroccan lamb wrap	301
fingers with minced lamb	117	lamb sticks	152	muesli bars	179
sh bites	89	lemon and garlic chicken	50	mushroom sauce	362
ffy eggs	133	lemon chicken wrap	266	new york roast wrap	289
ffy omelette	17	lemon pepper tuna melt	226	niçoise wrap	253
rest berry magic	360	light and lovely salmon wrap	275	nifty nachos	167
nch sandwich	54	light baked fish	32	noodle salad	344
sh oysters, 4 ways	84	linguini with breadcrumbs	26	olive and anchovy melt	224
sh salsa	348	little bacon and egg tarts	136	open burger melt	219
it bubble slice	180	little chicken and mushroom pies	99	pan-fried garlic prawns	85
ity pan scones	356	little snags with yummy sauce	164	paris best	239
rlic prawn and lime wrap	274	marinated mix tartlets	108	pasta bake	313
rmanic delight	215	marinated vegetable wrap	252	pastrami and beetroot melt	237
rman sausage and roesti	60	master soy fish	339	pastrami delight	299
anny's apple pancakes	354	meatballs with pasta	157	pepperoni and asparagus wrap	290
m, cheese and olive wrap	287	meat lover's melt	218	pineapple and carrot muffins	168
m, cheese and tomato melt	197	meat lover's pizza	322	pineapple and confetti cheese melt	234
m and mushroom melt	196	mexican chicken melt	208	pizza fingers	159
arty stew	314	mexican roll-ups	148	pizza muffins	161

367

index

pizza patties	162	smoked salmon bagel	41	traditional bruschetta	30
pork and vegetable skewers	109	smoked salmon gourmet wrap	279	traditional sausage rolls	112
potato and bacon turkish	61	smoked salmon on garlic toast	88	tropical delight	241
potato and beef rissoles	62	smoked trout melt	229	tuna and cheese rissoles	172
prawn and pineapple melt	224	smoked trout pasta	38	tuna and chilli melt	231
prawn cocktail wrap	278	smoked trout salad	35	tuna and mixed onion melt	232
prawn mornay melt	227	spicy cauliflower flowerettes	77	tuna and watercress salad	42
prawn omelette	342	steak and mushroom treat	221	tuna and watercress wrap	282
quesadillas	51	sticky tofu wrap	257	turkey, brie and avocado melt	210
raw energy wrap	255	stuffed capsicum boats	110	turkey, cranberry and avocado wrap	284
rhubarb and apple	354	stuffed mushrooms	111	turkey and cranberry melt	242
rich and tasty pork chops	321	stuffed zucchini	122	turkey and mango wrap	262
rissole parmigiana	150	supreme bolognese	320	turkey and pesto wrap	270
roast chicken and asparagus wrap	267	sushi flavours	230	turkey and special sauce melt	209
roast pork delight	222	sweet and mild chicken wrap	268	tuscan meatballs	114
roast pork with special sauce wrap	291	sweetcorn and bacon fritters	139	warm steak wrap	300
salmon and celery melt	228	sweet potato and cummin cubes	79	whole thai fish	338
salmon and spinach quiche	15	tangy chicken wrap	269	yoghurt muesli slice	182
salmon chats with dill cream	86	tangy tuna wrap	281	yummy baked spaghetti	140
saucy smoked fish	340	tasty fish mornay	39	zucchini fritters	80
sausage and veggie rolls	169	tasty green omelette	19		
sausage croquettes	170	tasty quiche parcels	20		
sausage melt	200	tasty tuna and mini penne	37		
savoury chicken croissant	240	thai chicken meatballs	102		
savoury tart	27	thai chicken meatballs	330		
scrambled tofu	28	thai fish bites	82		
seafood soup	341	thai fish wrap	272		
sesame burger wrap	259	tiny salmon tarts	90		
sesame honey prawn sticks	87	tiny topless bolognese pies	171		
smoked chicken and cucumber canapés	97	toad in the hole	352		
smoked ham and parsley salad wrap	256	tofu burgers	29		